COUNTRY FURNITURE FOR THE HOME

The Living Room

COUNTRY FURNITURE FOR THE HOME

The Living Room

TIMELESS TRADITIONAL
WOODWORKING PROJECTS

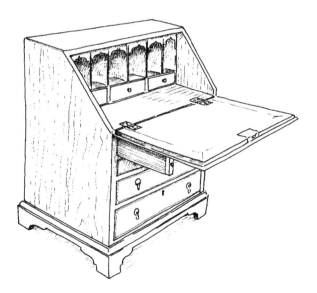

George Buchanan

CASSELL

Dedication
For David and Barbara Pilch

Acknowledgements
I should like to thank all my family and friends who have been
generous with their advice and criticism in the creation of this book.

Disclaimer
While every care has been taken over the accuracy of the information in
this book, the author and Publisher cannot be held responsible for any
accident related to products used by readers or to their workmanship.

A CASSELL BOOK
First published 1996 by Cassell, Wellington House
125 Strand, London WC2R 0BB

Copyright © 1996 George Buchanan
Photographs by Peter Harding

Distributed in the United States
by Sterling Publishing Co., Inc.
387 Park Avenue South, New York, NY 10016–8810

Distributed in Australia
by Capricorn Link (Australia) Pty Ltd
2/13 Carrington Road, Castle Hill, NSW 2154

British Library Cataloguing-in-Publication Data
A catalogue record for this book may be obtained from the British Library

ISBN 0–304–34241–6
Designed by Richard Carr
Printed and bound in Great Britain by The Bath Press

CONTENTS

INTRODUCTION

This is the second book in a series in which I describe how to make items of country furniture for the home.

Country furniture is made from solid wood. Sometimes it is made from pine, sometimes from locally grown hardwoods. It is traditional in style and substantially, if rather simply, constructed.

The ancestor of the armchair is Scandinavian, the design for the mirror comes from New England, the bureau and the joint stool are traditional English designs, while the couch is in the style of the Arts and Crafts Movement. The side table is provincial French.

I hope that when you look through these pages, you will not be discouraged by the apparent complexity of these pieces. They will all take some time to make, and, of course, the more parts there are and the more joints there are to make, the longer the job will take. But my workmanship is far from perfect – these pieces have been made quickly, and if you scrutinize the photographs you will see what I mean. In addition, furniture has always been built against the clock – how else would a country carpenter make his living? – so do not be despondent if your joints are not very good, and if you really feel depressed by the quality of your work, wander round an antique store specializing in country furniture and look closely at the work of your predecessors. I think most woodworkers will be comforted and inspired by such an experience.

In order to make these pieces you will need good quality wood-working tools. Carpentry is a very physical occupation. If you have good, well-maintained tools, the work will be a pleasure. If your tools are uncomfortable to hold and are blunt, using them will be difficult and unpleasant.

You will probably need five chisels (including one morticing chisel), a set square, two hand saws and a tenon saw, and a couple of planes. You will also need three or four C-clamps, a furniture clamp or two, and as many cheap spring clamps as you can find. A marking gauge, angle bevel, hammer, some punches and a screwdriver practically complete the list.

You will also need some power tools. Most people have an electric drill, but you will find a router invaluable, and a good quality jig saw is essential for some of these projects. Sanders, a circular saw and an electric planer will expedite matters, but they are not essential. I am not qualified to make judgements about the relative merits of the different brands of DIY power tools. I tend to buy Bosch tools. I enjoy using them and have always found them robust and reliable.

If you are going to make the joint stool, you will need access to a lathe. A range of high quality woodturner's lathes is available at surprisingly low prices. In my own workshop I have a converted treadle lathe that I bought in an auction, and also a small lathe, manufactured by Wolfcraft, which is driven by an electric drill and can be clamped to the work bench. This is a practical alternative to a purpose-built cast iron model. I have included instructions on using a lathe on page 28.

You will, of course, also need to buy wood. All these pieces, with the exception of the mirror, were made from timber that was cut locally. It is well worth while exploring your neighbourhood timber yards, from which you will be able to obtain woods that are far more beautiful and pleasant to use than the softwoods on sale in the large DIY stores. If you do not have access to wood yards or carpenters who will plane up the wood for you, these readily available, sized and planed timbers will be quite satisfactory.

Having all these items of equipment and the wood to hand you will need only time – the time that you are prepared to give to the piece you decide to make. And you will need a lot of it. But if you enjoy making things, I hope that these old designs will be an inspiration and my instructions a help.

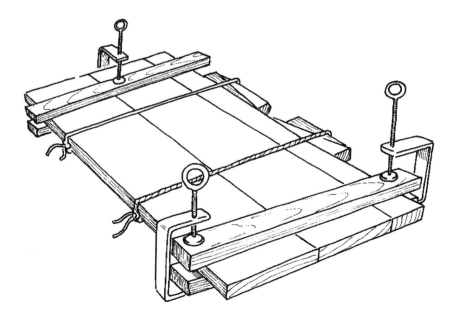

SEWING BOX

This small sewing box is made from pear wood. It has a hinged lid, and inside there are two trays. Pear wood is a heavy, silky-textured pink wood, which is pleasant to work but quite difficult to obtain. I was given the wood by a tree surgeon who had chopped down the tree because the trunk was rotten. Although the trunk was over 7ft (2.1m) long and 18in (about 460mm) in diameter, I was scarcely able to find enough wood to finish the box. The top and nearly all the sides are joined to make up the necessary widths.

The original box, on which I based this copy, was made of pine and painted with an uneven layer of red ochre paint. You can use any timber, but it is such a plain little thing that you should think ahead to how it will look when it is polished. A good finish will transform this basic box into something special.

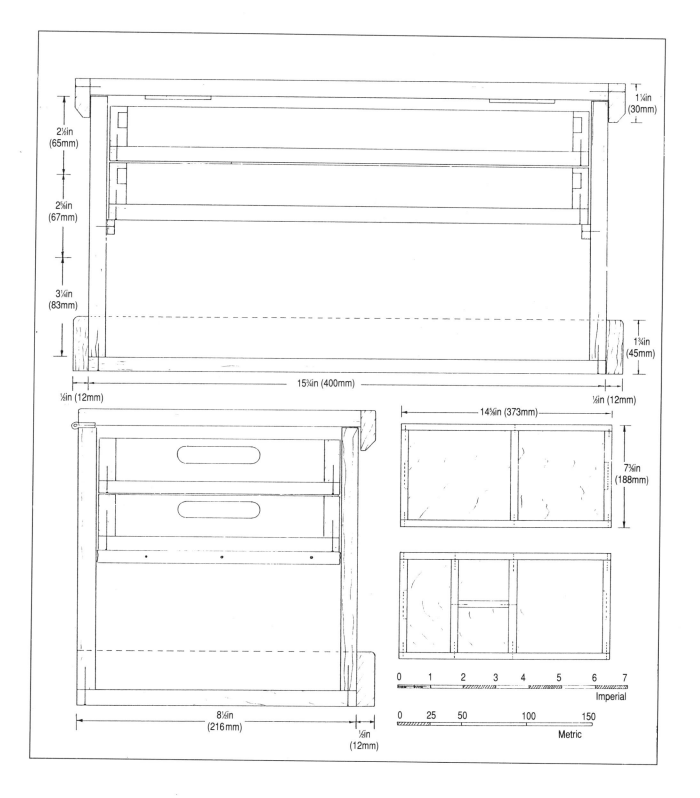

1¼in (30mm)

2½in (65mm)

2⅝in (67mm)

3¼in (83mm)

1¾in (45mm)

15¾in (400mm)

½in (12mm)

½in (12mm)

14⅝in (373mm)

7⅜in (188mm)

8½in (216mm)

½in (12mm)

0 1 2 3 4 5 6 7
Imperial

0 25 50 100 150
Metric

Fig. 1

The front, back and sides are dovetailed together, with through dovetails. The bottom is nailed to the underside of the sides, and the edges of the bottom are concealed by the moulding, which is nailed and glued around the base. The top is made from a plank, edged by a rim to hold the top flat. Neither the rim nor the base moulding continues across the back of the box (Fig. 1).

Through dovetails are quite difficult to cut neatly. I have included instructions here to help in cutting and fitting them, and if you follow these guidelines and use sharp tools, the results should be excellent. If they are not, you can always fill the gaps in the joints and hope no one will notice.

CONSTRUCTION

The sides, top and mouldings are all cut from ½in (12mm) thick wood. If it were much thicker, cutting the dovetails would be tedious; if it were thinner, the box would be flimsy.

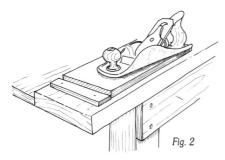

Fig. 2

To start you should plane your wood flat and thickness it to ½in (12mm) thick. Most professional carpenters and joiners have a thicknesser in their workshops and will not charge much to machine your wood to the right thickness. Make sure there are no nails in it. If you would rather not use the services of a machine workshop, plane the pieces by hand in the following order.

Saw the components of the box roughly to size. Arrange an end stop on your bench (Fig. 2) and plane one surface of each piece flat. You can test how flat it is by placing parallel sided winding sticks at each end of the plank and sighting down them (Fig. 3). Shave away the high spots until the top of the plank is flat and smooth. (For advice on using and sharpening a plane see pages 153–4.)

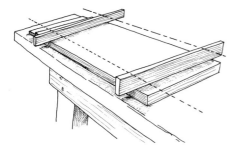

Fig. 3

Take a marking gauge and set it to ½in (12mm). Scribe around the edges of each board. Check that the surface of the bench where you will be planing the timber is flat and smooth and will not scratch the surface you have already finished. Place each component in turn face down on the bench and plane them down to the scribe line.

The planks for the top and sides need to be at least 9in (229mm) wide, and you may find it necessary to join one or two pieces to make up the widths.

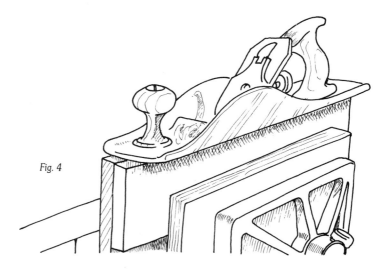

Fig. 4

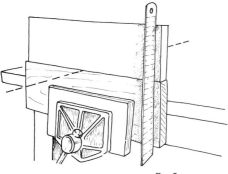

Fig. 5

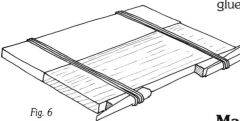

Fig. 6

Saw the additional pieces roughly to size and plane them to a little over ½in (12mm) thick. Place the pairs that are to be joined together in the vice, one pair at a time, and use a long try plane to true the edges (Fig. 4; see also page 151). Check the joint by placing them together in position, as illustrated in Fig. 5. They should be plumb with each other, and no light should be visible between them when seen from the side. If you find it difficult to achieve a good joint, try rubbing blackboard chalk on the joining edge of the strip that is not in the vice. Lower this on to the edge of the piece in the vice and rub it lengthways a short distance. Take a shoulder plane and smooth away the chalk marks left on the piece held in the vice. If you check regularly and remove only the finest shavings, you will achieve a good join.

Glue the pieces together using white PVA glue. Hold them in position with string and opposing wedges (Fig. 6). When the glue has dried, smooth the surfaces with a plane.

Cut each piece to size. Add no more than ⅛in (4mm) to the overall length of the sides before cutting them, and the same for the ends. Plane the top and bottom edges straight and exactly to width.

Marking and cutting the dovetails

Take the front and the backboards, align their edges, and tack them together using a pair of panel pins. Align and tack the sides in the same way.

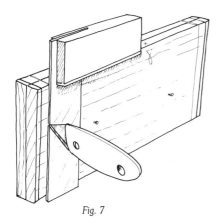

Fig. 7

SHOULDER-LINES

Use a set square and a sharp pencil to mark in the ends of the two pairs of planks. Square around each end so that the marks are transferred to the sides and edges of each piece at each end (Fig. 7). You will not be able to transfer the mark to the inside, touching faces at present. Mark the shoulder-lines for the dovetails and pins with a marking knife at the same time. The marks at the end of each pair of planks should look as illustrated in Fig. 8.

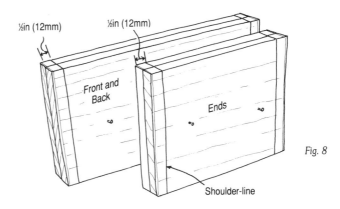

½in (12mm)   ½in (12mm)

Front and Back

Ends

Shoulder-line

Fig. 8

ARRANGING AND MARKING DOVETAILS

The dovetails are cut into the ends of the front and back plank and are marked and cut first (Fig. 9). When the tails have been cut, the pins can be marked and the joint fitted together.

I arranged and drew the dovetails free-hand, but it is just as easy and almost as fast to measure the spaces with a ruler or dividers and to mark the tails with a simple cardboard template (Fig. 10). Square across the ends of the boards.

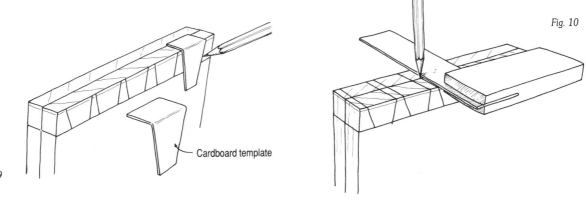

Fig. 10

Cardboard template

Fig. 9

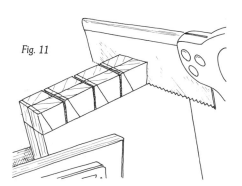

Fig. 11

SAWING

Place the boards in the vice, at the slight angle shown, then use a tenon saw to cut down all the perpendicular lines, stopping at the shoulder-line (Fig. 11). Change the angle of the boards in the vice and saw down the second set of marks.

Re-arrange the board in the vice, and carefully remove the waste from the edges of the end dovetails with a tenon saw (Fig. 12). Trim exactly to the shoulder-line with a sharp chisel if necessary (Fig. 13). Now place the planks, still nailed together, on a flat board of waste wood, and use a mallet and a ¼in (6mm) bevel-edged chisel to chop out the waste from between the tails (Fig. 14). Remove small quantities at a time. Make sure

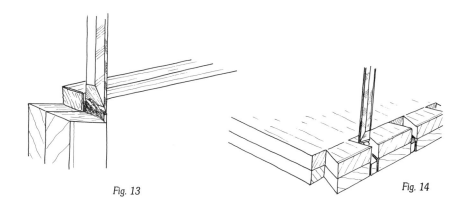

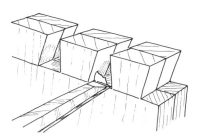

Fig. 12

Fig. 13

Fig. 14

Fig. 15

that the chisel is vertical in both planes as you chop downwards, and only try to chisel part way through the two boards. When you have removed the waste from between the tails on one side, turn the board over and repeat on the other side. Place the board end up in the vice and trim across the shoulders to finish (Fig. 15).

If you have found this difficult, you should first check that your chisel is sharp. (For instructions on sharpening see page 153.) If the chisel is sharp and you are still worried about cutting the tails, you can prise the two planks apart with a wide chisel or a plane blade, and mark in the missing shoulder-lines on the facing sides. Now remove the waste from one plank at a time. This will be easier, but it will still have been worth nailing them together, because it makes it possible to complete the marking and sawing quickly.

Separate the side planks and complete the marking of the shoulder-lines with a marking knife. Pencil identifying marks on the top edge, inside face and outside face of each side, and arrange all four planks (the sides, front and back) in their appropriate position relative to each other on the bench. While they are in position, number or letter each row of dovetails with their matching side (Fig. 16). This avoids confusion later.

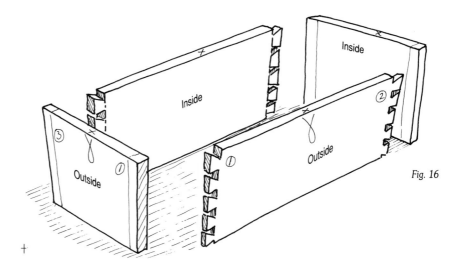

Fig. 16

MARKING AND CUTTING THE PINS

The pins are wedge-shaped, and they are cut into the ends of the sides. They taper towards the outside face (Fig. 17).

Cut one of the back set of pins first. You can cut the front ones last, when you have experimented and perfected your skills. Place the side vertically in the vice, with the edge into which you will be cutting the pins flush with the top of the vice and its outside face facing away from the bench.

Place the dovetails in position over the side, top edges aligned and face side upwards. Before marking the pins, move the dovetails across a little in the direction shown (Fig. 18). Press the dovetails against the side, and use a knife or a fine saw blade to incise the tails (Fig. 19). You will notice that the effect of moving the dovetails sideways is to mark the pins a little larger than they need to be. The benefit of this is that if your lines are clear and well incised, you can lodge your dovetail saw in each line and cut down it, leaving a row of pins the exact size required.

Fig. 17

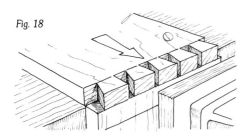

Fig. 18

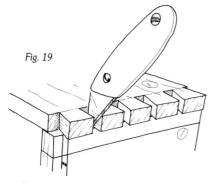

Fig. 19

Overlap exaggerated

You will need to experiment a little to find the ideal offset. This will vary according not only to the width of cut made by your dovetail saw but also to the hardness of the wood you are cutting. If the wood is hard, like pear or oak, you will have to use a slightly smaller offset because it will not compress readily when the dovetails are fitted. If you are using a fairly soft and springy wood, like spruce or cherry, you can have a larger offset and expect the pins to compress a little as the dovetails are driven home.

When you have marked the first row of pins, remove the dovetails and lift the side upwards in the vice so that the shoulder-line is above the level of the vice jaws. Take the dovetail saw, hold the blade vertically, place it on the first mark and saw down to the shoulder-line. Repeat with the other marks (Fig. 20).

Fig. 20

When all the pins on this first end have been sawn, hold the side in the vice, with the pins upwards, and use a coping saw to remove most of the waste (Fig. 21). Next, lay the side on a piece of flat wood and, using a mallet and ⅝in (15mm) chisel, chop away the waste between the pins. Remember to hold the chisel vertically and to remove small chips at a time. Turn the board over to finish off. In the final cut, if the chisel is lodged in the incised shoulder-line and is angled slightly into the edge of the timber (Fig. 22), the dovetails will bed snugly against the shoulder.

Before fitting them together, pare away the inside corners of the dovetails (Fig. 23). This helps the dovetails to slide between the pins.

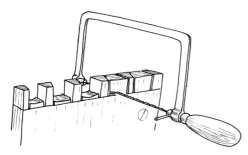

Fig. 21

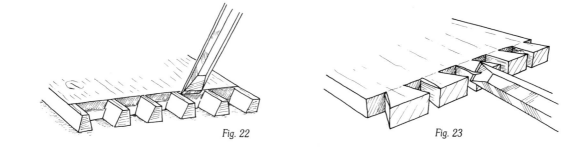

Fig. 22

Fig. 23

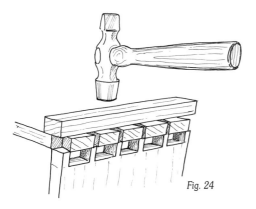

Fig. 24

FITTING THE DOVETAILS

Place the dovetails over the pins, which you can hold in the vice. Inspect the joint. If the dovetails fall into position, it will be because you made the pins too small, and the remedy next time is to offset the dovetail a little more than you did this time.

If you can press the dovetails into position easily, the joint will look a little ragged, so next time, you should offset the tails a fraction more to make the pins a little bit wider.

If you can almost press the tails into position, place a batten across the top of the tails, and tap them in with a light hammer (Fig. 24). Work carefully and watch the pins at each end, because they might split if the fit is too tight or if the sides of the pins have not been cut vertically. Once the joint is assembled, you can separate it by placing a batten in the corner on the inside, lift the side just clear of the bench, and tap the batten lightly with a hammer (Fig. 25).

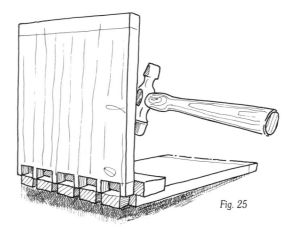

Fig. 25

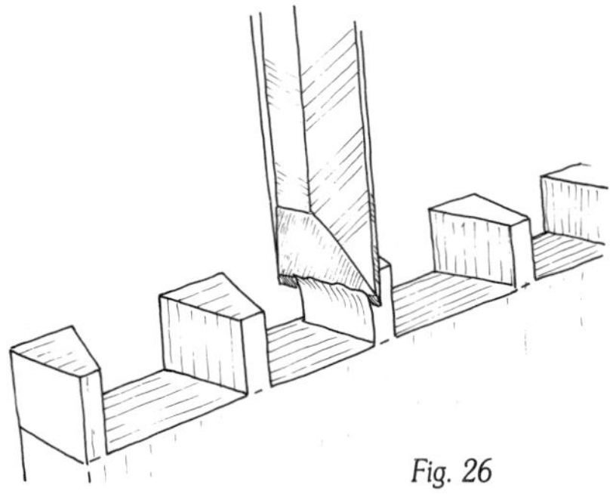

If the tails are obviously not going to fit, trim the pins carefully with a chisel (Fig. 26). Make sure that the sides of the pins are trimmed vertical. It is difficult to drive the dovetails home if the pins broaden as they reach the shoulder-line.

Tap the dovetails into the pins and inspect your work. The ends of the tails and pins should be a little prominent, and they will have to be planed flush with the sides and front with a sharp shoulder plane. Any blemishes in the joints can be filled after the box is glued together.

Now mark and cut the pins for the opposite side of the back, and then mark and cut the pins for the dovetails at the front of the box.

Fig. 26

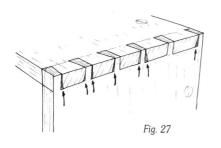

Fig. 27

Problems with dovetails

The illustrations show some typical faults, and are accompanied with hints for avoiding them.

- The dovetails show gaps where they have not been cut square (Fig. 27). Use a set square to mark out pairs before cutting.

- The sides split where dovetails have been forced in (Fig. 28). Check the pins with a set square.

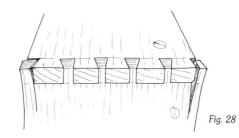

Fig. 28

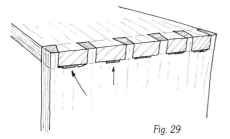

Fig. 29

- The shoulder-lines are eaten away by a chisel (Fig. 29). Incise the line clearly with a sharp knife and use the chisel most carefully when you chop out the waste.

- The pins are too small. Increase offset as indicated (Fig. 30).

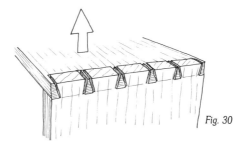

Fig. 30

- The sides of the dovetails are raggedly sawn (Fig. 31). Sharpen your saw or use a saw with a finer blade. If you do not have a fine-toothed dovetail saw, a small metal hack saw will do instead.

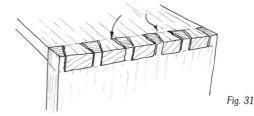

Fig. 31

ASSEMBLY

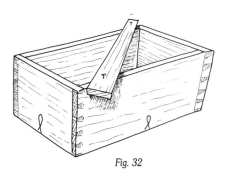

Fig. 32

When all four joints have been cut – and you can expect this to take at least 2 hours to complete – separate the pieces, run a little white woodworker's glue on to the sides of the pins and the chiselled recesses between them and assemble the joints. Tap them tight, resting the box on two battens as you tap the dovetails home. Check that the box is square, and if it needs holding square while the glue dries, tack a diagonal batten across the underside (Fig. 32). Wipe away any excess glue on the inside of the box with a damp rag.

Fitting the bottom

The bottom is glued and tacked straight on to the edges of the box. When the glue holding the joints is set, take a shoulder plane and gently smooth across the joints on the underside of the box to make it level.

Hold the box in the vice and plane up the dovetails. Then plane the bottom board until it is flush with the sides and front. Use a shoulder plane for this, and where you are trimming the end-grain, plane inwards from the corners to avoid splitting the edges of the plank (Fig. 33).

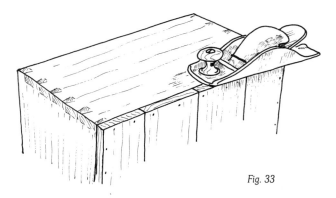

Fig. 33

Fitting the base moulding

The base moulding is a simple strip of ½in (12mm) thick wood, 1¾in (45mm) wide, with a bevel planed on its top edge. The moulding extends across the front and down each side, but it does not cover the back. It is fitted flush with the bottom of the box, and is glued to the front and sides. The corners are mitred (Fig. 34).

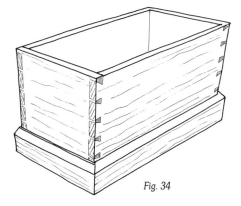

Fig. 34

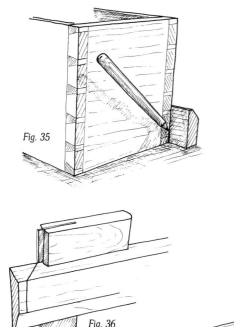

Fig. 35

Fig. 36

You will need about 38in (965mm) of moulding for the box. This is because each mitre will take an additional inch (25mm). To be safe, cut more than required. Before you cut the strip into pieces for the front and sides, mark and plane the bevel on its top edge.

Mark the front length first. Hold it in position on the front of the box with a little more than ½in (12mm) overhanging the box at one end. Pencil in a line showing the box corner on the top edge of the moulding (Fig. 35) and then tuck the pencil behind the moulding and draw a line on the moulding to mark the side of the box. Remove the moulding. With the set square, resting against the underside of the moulding, square up the pencil line on the inside face.

Take an angle bevel set to 45 degrees (or make your own cardboard template), and mark the mitres at each end on the underside of the moulding, and square up at the front (Fig. 36). The marks on the moulding should resemble those in Fig. 37.

Now place the moulding in the vice, at a slight angle, and saw down the end mitre using a tenon saw (Fig. 38).

Fig. 37

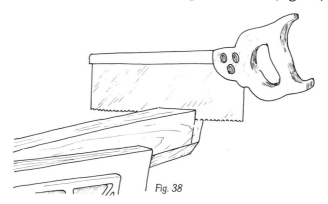

Fig. 38

It might help the saw to get started if you relieve the line on the base of the moulding with a chisel before sawing (Fig. 39).

Fig. 39

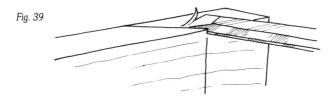

In order to cut square you need to saw slowly and lightly. Try to keep your arm moving in a parallel motion, while the hand holding the saw handle keeps the blade from leaning off line. Provided you have a sharp saw and work slowly, you should not have any trouble. If you have to wander off line, try to wander off on the waste side. It is then a simple matter to place the moulding in the vice and trim the mitre flat with a shoulder plane (Fig. 40).

Fig. 40

If you wander the other way, you will need to mark the entire joint again before trimming it flat.

When your first mitre is cut, pass the shoulder plane over its face twice, lightly, to remove any raggedness, and then hold it in position and draw in the marks for the other end. If everything is in order, cut the second mitre. Once you have cut it, it may be necessary to trim it to its exact length with the shoulder plane. If you have to do this, check your planing very frequently, because it is easy to spoil a mitre in this way.

Mark and cut the mitre of one of the return mouldings. Leave a little waste at the back end and saw it off; mark and cut the second mitre for the other side. These two side pieces are fitted after the front moulding is nailed and glued in position.

Tip the box on its back and place the front moulding in position on it. Check the mitres again to make sure they are exactly right, then drive a veneer pin through the moulding close to each corner and near to the bottom edge. Stop hammering the pins when their points just poke through the back face of the moulding, this will supply a grip to help position and hold the moulding while it is glued. Hold the moulding in position on the box and carefully press it in place.

Apply glue to the inside face of the moulding, and then slide the moulding upwards into position (Fig. 41). You should feel when the pins locate in the dents they made earlier.

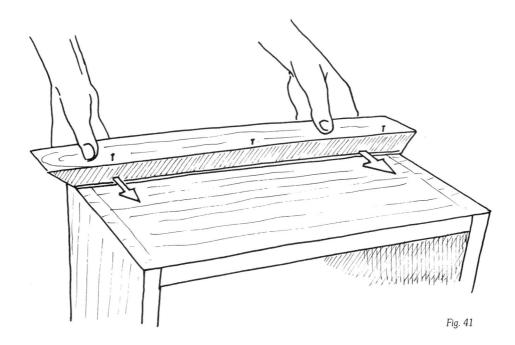

Fig. 41

Wipe away any glue that obscures the joints and inspect each end. If everything is satisfactory, hammer in the pins until they are almost flush with the front of the moulding. Hammer in some extra pins to help hold the moulding in place. Tap their heads below the surface with a fine nail punch. Wipe away any surplus glue with a wet rag and leave it to dry.

When the glue is dry, lift the box on to its base and fit the two side mouldings. These are easy to fit – you only have to press the moulding against the mitres at the front and trim away those bits that prevent a good tight fit. Take care that you do not cut away so much that the side pieces are not long enough. Nail and glue them in position and bind the mitre with masking tape to hold it closed until the glue is dry. Trim the side mouldings to length later.

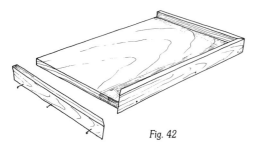

Fig. 42

The top

The top needs to be about ⅛in (4mm) deeper and a fraction wider than the box so that the lip moulding clears the top of the box when it is opened. Cut the top to size and plane its sides straight and square. Cut and fit the lip moulding in exactly the same way as the base moulding was fitted (Fig. 42).

Fitting the hinges

The hinges are screwed to the flat top of the box and into shallow recesses chiselled in the back of the box.

Screw the hinges to the top first. They are positioned at the very back of the top, about 2in (50mm) in from each side (Fig. 43). Screw them in place with short countersunk brass screws.

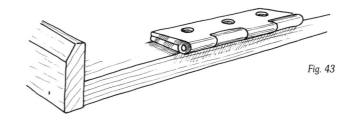

Fig. 43

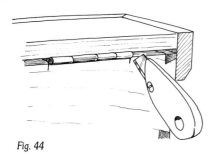

Fig. 44

Place the lid on the box and mark the positions of the hinges on the back of the box with a marking knife (Fig. 44).

Remove the lid and square across the top of the back plank with a knife and set square. Set your marking gauge to a little under the full depth of the hinge. Use the gauge to scribe between the marks at each hinge location (Fig. 45).

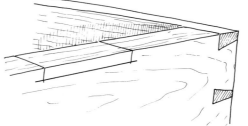

Fig. 45

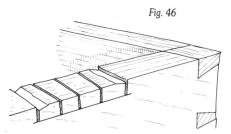
Fig. 46

Place the box in the vice, back plank facing towards you, and relieve the lines at the ends of each hinge recess. Saw down at each line to the scribe line. Make a few additional saw cuts between them to weaken the waste (Fig. 46).

Clamp a batten inside the box. This will stiffen the backboard and prevent it from splitting. Pare away the waste wood with a very sharp chisel (Fig. 47).

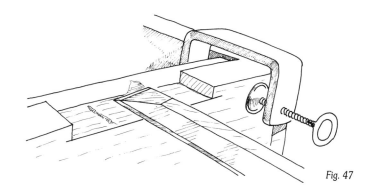
Fig. 47

When you have finished both recesses, put the lid in position, and when you have obtained a clear idea of where the hinge should be set by inspecting the back of the box, screw the hinges in place.

The trays

There are two trays in this box. The lower one rests on two battens glued and tacked to the sides of the box. The second tray sits on top of the lower one.

Plane up a 16in (405mm) strip of batten, about ¼in (6mm) wide and ½in (12mm) deep. Cut it to length so that the pieces slip into place inside the box. In addition, cut a short rectangular strip of hardboard or waste wood, 3¾in (95mm) wide and 5–7in (127–180mm) long. This spacer guide saves marking and helps to position the battens when you are nailing them in place.

Drive a couple of gimp or veneer pins into each batten, leaving them with their points just poking through, and spread glue on the first batten. Tip the box on end. Support the side with a piece of waste wood, slip the spacer guide piece into the box where it should rest on the side and touch the base. Now put the batten inside, push it against the guide and nail it in place (Fig. 48). Repeat at the other end.

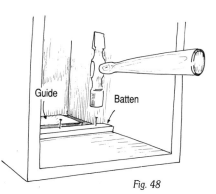
Guide   Batten
Fig. 48

Cut and trim the two tray bases to size, and saw and plane up enough wood for the rims and dividers. The construction of these trays is very simple. The sides and ends are nailed to the base, then the corners are nailed together. The ends fit between the sides, and they must be cut exactly to length.

Fit the long sides first. It will help if you drive a few veneer pins through the base to prevent the pieces slipping around when the joint is being glued. Trim them to length.

Cut the sides to fit, and rout a finger grip on the inside face of each end piece. (For advice on using a router see pages 55, 92 and 117.) Fit and glue the end pieces (Fig. 49).

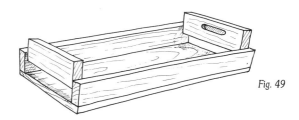

Fig. 49

Fig. 50

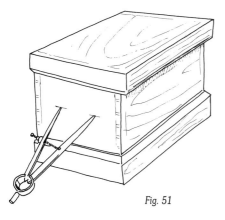

Fig. 51

This small-scale work can be accomplished easily and accurately using the right angle guide on the circular saw bench. Pre-drill and then nail each corner with a couple of 1½in (38mm) panel pins.

Fit the partitions in the same way.

Now is the time to bore the holes for the brass handles at the sides. Most good ironmongers will supply brass swan neck handles illustrated (Fig. 50). To fit them, lay them out, with the handle held at each end by the cupped bolts. Set a pair of dividers to record the centres of the two bolts. The bolts for the handles are inserted just below the light battens that support the trays. Use a set square to mark the level for the handles and mark the positions for the bolt holes with the points of the dividers (Fig. 51).

FINISHING

Punch the nails that hold the base and lid moulding below the surface of the wood and fill any holes, cracks and blemishes with two-part wood filler. Remove the brass hinges and take out the trays.

Sand the box with 180 grit paper, then scrape it lightly with a cabinet scraper. Dust it and then brush it all over with a fairly strong solution of tannic acid (dissolved in water) and leave it to dry.

Fume the box and lid (but not the trays) by leaving them for 4 hours in a clear polythene bag containing a dish of ammonia dissolved in water. Remove them and leave them until they lose their terrible pungent smell. Fuming the box in ammonia will darken the wood from a light pink to a deep brown. (For further information about fuming see page 50.)

Sand the inside and outside of the box with 220 open cut sandpaper and stain the wood with a mixture of English Light Oak, American Walnut and some Canadian Cedar Colron stain. This warms up the colour of the wood.

Leave the box to dry, then use watercolour paint to disguise any fillers that have not taken the stain adequately, adding a little soap to the brush to make the paint hold.

When the paint is dry, brush a dilute coat of button polish over the outside and inside of the box. Then continue on the outside to apply a rubbed coat of French polish, using shellac. (For instructions on this finishing schedule see pages 138–40.)

Fitting the handles

The handles are fitted before the box is rubbed down and waxed. After polishing leave the box for a day or two for the shellac to harden. Then take the handles and insert them into the sides of the box.

After you have tightened the nuts, reach inside with a small hack saw, and start a shallow cut into each bolt right next to the nut. Now remove the handles and bolts, replace the nuts on the bolts, and, holding the bolts in the vice, saw off the surplus thread. Hold the waste thread in the vice, with the nut wound up the thread close to the cup. When the waste has been removed, you will find that as you unscrew the nut, it will straighten out and repair any small damage that the thread has suffered in being cut.

Insert and fasten the handles and screw the hinges back on.

Waxing

Take some 000 wire wool and gather it in a bunch. Lightly rub it all over the box to remove its glitter. Now apply a cloth loaded with soft brown wax polish to the exterior of the box. Use a soft cloth to remove the excess and leave the wax to harden. After a short while, burnish the box with a soft woollen cloth.

OAK JOINT STOOL

The stool in the photograph is a copy of an oak Jacobean stool. It stands 22in (about 560mm) high, and the top is 22in (about 560mm) long and 13½in (about 345mm) wide. The centre portions of the legs are turned to a gun-barrel shape. The top, the rails beneath the top and the stretchers are decorated with hand-carved mouldings.

This stool is constructed with glued and pegged mortice and tenon joints. Hidden tenons join the top, which is pegged to the framework. Seen from the ends, the legs taper towards the top. Seen from the front and back, however, the legs are vertical. This does not add to the difficulty of making the stool, however, because the mortices in the legs are all cut in the same way, while the shoulders of the end rails and stretchers are cut at an angle and the tenons are trimmed to fit.

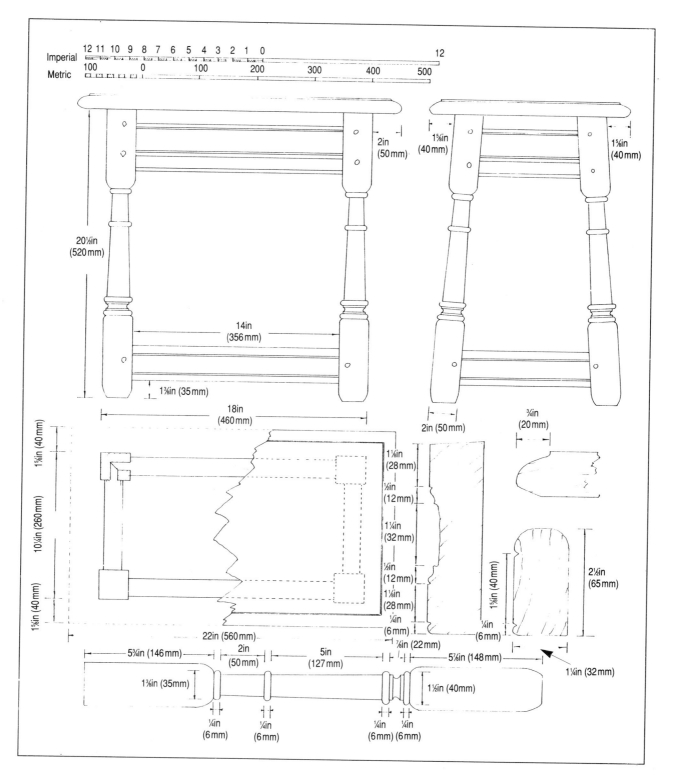

I have deliberately antiqued the finish and included some suggestions for those who would like to do the same to theirs. Apart from sawing the components roughly to size with a circular saw and turning the legs on an electric lathe, everything else has been done with hand tools. I did not use any sandpaper except for finishing the turnings. The result is a stool that is a little rough and crude in places and that looks old. We are used to seeing modern furniture with impeccable, smooth surfaces and perfect joints. Here the top is left scalloped by the plane iron, the mouldings on the rails are uneven and crude, exactly as they were carved. I am pleased with the result, and the instructions explain the woodworking techniques I used.

CONSTRUCTION

I made this stool from oak, but any fruit wood would be as attractive. Ash would also be suitable, although pine or fir will not look as pleasing, unless the stool is painted or cleverly 'antiqued'.

Saw the components to size. In the stool featured in the drawings, the top is made from two pieces joined edge to edge to make up the width. The join need not be in the centre – it is more important that you choose a particularly attractive piece of timber. Add pieces to bring it to size.

The legs are turned from 2in (50mm) square rough sawn oak, 22in (about 560mm) long. They are trimmed to length after the joints are finished. The rails are 4½in (115mm) deep and about 1in (25mm) thick, and the stretchers are a little over 2in (50mm) deep. While you are sawing the pieces, look out for an offcut of straight-grained wood from which you can split the pegs.

Turning the legs

Take a scrap of wood 23in (about 585mm) long and pencil on it the positions for the turned features on the leg. Mark the position of the top of the leg about 1in (25mm) in from the end, then the top shoulder and first bead, the second bead, then the two beads and cove at the other end of the barrel. The lower line of the bottom bead also marks the top shoulder of the unturned lower part of the leg (Fig. 1).

Unless you are familiar with woodturning, I suggest you now take a scrap of waste wood, 2in (50mm) square and about 22in (560mm) long to practise on.

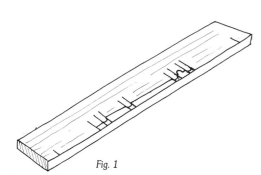

Fig. 1

Take your practice piece and mark the centres at its ends. Centre-punch where the lines cross. Transfer the marks from your turning guide on to the leg with a soft black pencil (Fig. 2).

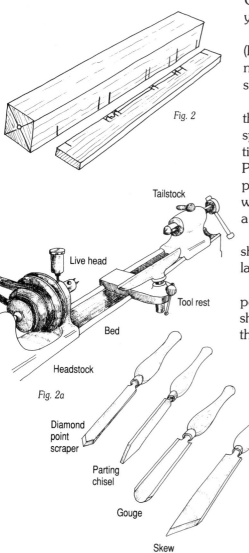

Fig. 2

Tailstock

Live head

Tool rest

Bed

Headstock

Fig. 2a

Diamond point scraper

Parting chisel

Gouge

Skew chisel

In addition to a lathe and the lathe tools described below (Fig. 2a), you will need one or two calipers or dividers. If you do not have any, make some out of ⅛in (4mm) plywood, and use a small bolt at the top so that they pivot.

Place the leg between the lathe centres, inserting the point of the live head in the centre-punch holes. Tap the leg into the drive spurs of the live head. Now move the tailstock into position and tighten its point into the centre-punch hole at the other end. Position the long tool rest so that it is level with the two centre points, parallel to the bed of the lathe and just clear of the leg when you rotate it slowly by hand. Select a moderate speed, squirt a little oil on the point of the tailstock and switch on the lathe.

Your pencil marks, which define the length of the turned part, should be visible as the leg rotates. If they are not, stop the lathe, and darken or extend them.

Take the diamond point scraper, hold it tightly and gingerly poke it into the revolving leg just on the waste side of the shoulder-line (Fig. 3). (The waste in this case is the area between the upper and lower shoulder marks.)

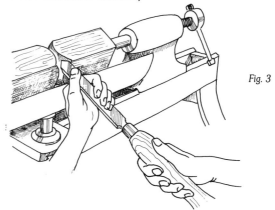

Fig. 3

At first the scraper will only be cutting away the corners of the leg. When you have pushed the point of the scraper inwards by about ⅜in (9mm), withdraw it and make a second cut immediately next to the first, on its waste side. As you widen the cut, there is less chance of the side of the scraper hitting and splintering the corners of the leg, and you can deepen the indentation you have made until the scraper makes a continuous cut right around the leg.

Now repeat this at the other end, remembering to keep to the waste side of the line.

Stop the lathe and inspect what you have done. Defining the turning area at each end should be a slightly splintery groove (Fig. 4). If the grooves are continuous, you can carry on; if they are not, scrape them a little deeper until they are.

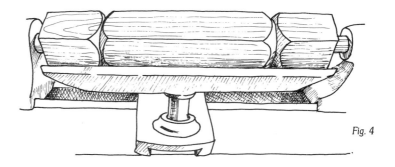

Fig. 4

Fig. 5

Start the lathe. Take the diamond point scraper again, hold it firmly against the tool rest and, with your right hand grasping the end of its long handle, move it along the tool rest from one groove towards the other. Move the tool slowly. Rough splinters will fly off, but they will not damage the ends of the leg. The danger in moving fast is that the point might cause the driving head to lose its grip, and you will then waste time re-establishing a satisfactory anchorage for it.

Use the point to reduce the area between the grooves to a cylinder. As the corners of the leg are chipped away by the scraper, you will notice that there is less vibration, and you can change tools and use a large gouge to finish this stage (Fig. 5).

Stop the motor. Set your first caliper to the dimension of the top bead, and your second to the greater setting of the bottom bead. Because the leg you want to turn is tapered, adjust the angle of the tool rest until it is the angle you want (Fig. 6). Before you switch on the lathe, check that the ends of the leg do not hit the rest.

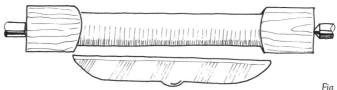

Fig. 6

The parting chisel is used to make a narrow groove at each end of the cylinder, and it registers the depth of cut necessary to make the taper. Set your calipers to the diameters of the top bead and bottom bead. Take the parting chisel. It is used on its edge and at right angles to the axis of the piece being turned. It has to be gripped very tightly with both hands. Stand sideways on and, if you are right-handed, hold the end of the handle with your right hand and press the edge of the blade against the tool rest with your left hand. Drop your right hand to lift the tip of the blade and align the chisel at right angles to the top shoulder-line (Fig. 7).

Fig. 7

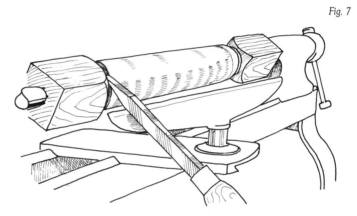

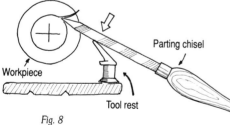

Fig. 8

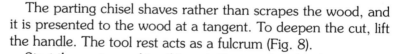
Parting chisel

The parting chisel shaves rather than scrapes the wood, and it is presented to the wood at a tangent. To deepen the cut, lift the handle. The tool rest acts as a fulcrum (Fig. 8).

Start the motor and try this out. Present the chisel cautiously, with its cutting edge above the revolving wood and slightly to the tool rest side of its axis when seen from above. Grip the tool against the tool rest and slowly lift the handle. As the chisel makes contact with the wood it will plane a smooth, square-sided groove around the leg.

This is a much easier tool to use than it might seem, and you must be careful that you do not get carried away and make your first cut deeper than you need. Switch off the motor and check the diameter of the channel with the calipers. Make a suitable groove at each end of the cylinder as a depth reference for turning the taper.

Start the motor and take a large gouge. Hold it on its side against the tool rest so that, with its curved cutting edge, it planes rather than scrapes the wood (compare this with the action shown in Fig. 5). Draw it down the taper and back, reversing its angle on the return journey. If you hold the gouge as illustrated in Figs. 9 and 10, you can use your hand as a fence to keep the cutting edge parallel to the tool rest. While you are using the gouge, take care to keep your hands clear of the sharp cornered ends of the leg. Do not press the gouge too hard into the wood. If you do, the leg will whip and the tool will bounce, leaving an irregular finish, which is difficult to smooth.

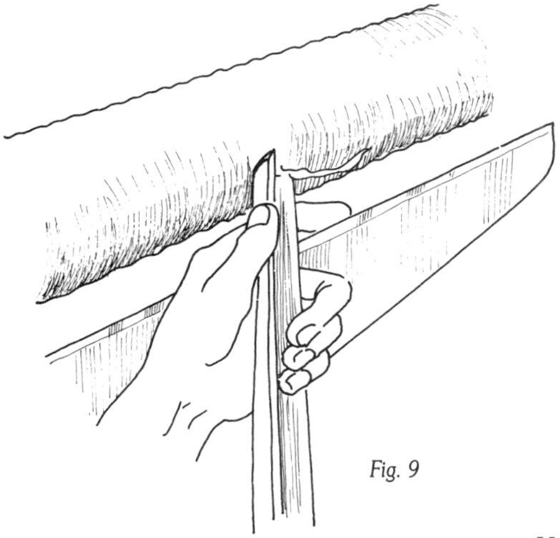

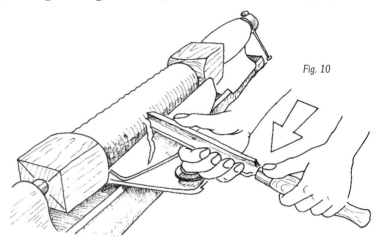

Fig. 10

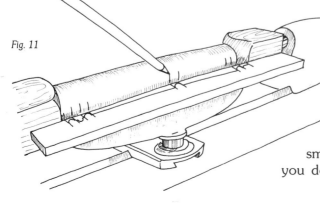

Fig. 9

When it is used in this way, the gouge provides a quick and easy means of reducing the diameter of the stock. Very soon you will be making rapid passes with the gouge, removing an almost continuous shaving of wood as you work. If you encounter knots, press the tool even more tightly against the rest, slow down its rate of travel along the rest and reduce the quantity of wood you are removing with each pass.

Switch off the lathe when you have completed turning the tapered cylinder.

Fig. 11

Take the measuring guide and transfer the salient features of the leg to the cylinder with a soft black pencil. The end shoulders are already well defined, but now you need to mark the positions of the four beads (Fig. 11). When they are marked, turn on the lathe and take the parting tool again. This time it is for cutting grooves at the sides of each bead so that the areas between the beads can be levelled and smoothed. If you look at Fig. 12 you will notice that you do not need a groove below the bottom bead (because this butts against the lower shoulder) or above the top bead (because this is cut from the end of a small length of cylinder left at the top).

Fig. 12

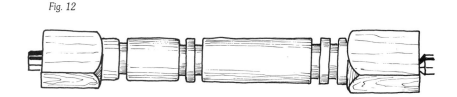

The beads themselves are radiused and are almost ¼in (6mm) in diameter, so the grooves defining them at each side should not be much more than ⅛in (4mm) deep.

Take the gouge again, and remove the long sections of waste from each side of the centre bead. Switch off the lathe and raise the tool rest until it is level with the top of the tapered turning.

Take the large skew chisel, hold it as illustrated in Fig. 13 and lay it flat on the side of the taper. Your left hand will control the movement along the rest, while your right hand steadies the tool. In addition, your right hand (which is at the end of the handle) controls the depth of cut by twisting the handle. Try this action with the lathe switched off. As the handle is twisted, the sharp cutting edge comes into contact with the wood, and,

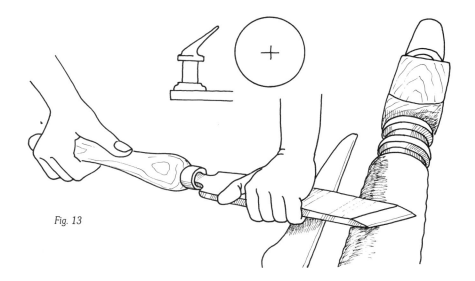

Fig. 13

provided that it is expected to cut only a fine shaving, it will leave a smooth, planed finish as it is drawn along the tool rest.

As with the gouge, the more pressure that is applied to the turning, the more likely it is to whip and cause the chisel to chatter and leave a rippled finish. To avoid this, tighten the tail-stock a little to remove sideways play, and remember that you can press as hard as you like on the tool rest as long as you can still move the chisel along it at the same time. It might help to ease the movement of the skew chisel along the rest if you file off its sharp edges (×).

Start the lathe and place the chisel on the turning mid-point between the beads, with the heel of the skew chisel touching the wood. Twist the chisel slowly until the heel cuts a fine shaving, then, keeping the angle constant, move the chisel along the rest until the heel reaches the bead (Fig. 14). Turn over the chisel and move it in the opposite direction to smooth the remainder. Choose a smaller skew and smooth the narrow area between the top and middle beads.

The beads are rounded with the small skew chisel. Switch off the lathe again and lay the chisel flat on the bead. To turn a bead with a small radius, simply twist the handle in a clockwise direction to cut the right-hand side of the bead, reverse the chisel and twist the handle in an anticlockwise direction to complete the other side (Fig. 15). The chisel does not move along the rest at all. The cutting is done with the heel of the chisel, and the only danger arises if you do not hold the tool tightly or if it is not at right angles to the axis of the turning, when the cutting edge might bite into the bead and veer sideways.

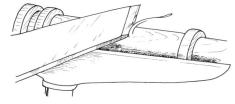

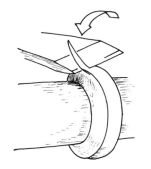

Fig. 14

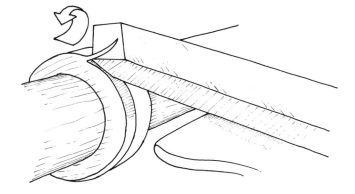

Fig. 15

Practise this movement a few times before turning on the lathe.

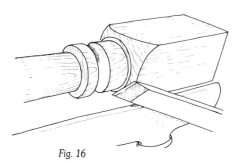

Fig. 16

The top bead needs to be separated from the rest of the short turning that is adjacent to the shoulder. To do this, lower the tool rest, hold the small skew chisel with its back edge resting on the tool rest (Fig. 16), keep the handle level and, in two slow, jabbing movements, cut a steep V to delineate the bead.

While the tool rest is still lowered, take the smallest gouge and, holding it on its side (just as the larger ones were held when they cleared away the waste to form the tapered cylinder), drive it firmly into the space between the two lower beads, turning the handle clockwise as you go until the gouge reaches the centre of the cove. At this point the gouge should be at right angles to the axis of the turning and level (Fig. 17). As long as you hold the thin gouge tightly, introduce its side into the cut and roll it level, it will cut a clean-sided cove. The other side of the cove can be cut by reversing the operation.

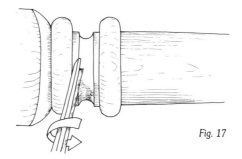

Fig. 17

Now raise the tool rest and complete turning the top bead with the skew chisel.

Stop the lathe and inspect what you have done. The shoulders at each end will probably need to be tidied. Use the diamond point scraper to do this. The rest of the leg should approximate to the drawing in the plans. This is the practice leg. If this is the first turning you have done, you will already have learnt quite a bit about turning. If you are disappointed with the result and worried about turning the legs, try sanding the leg while it is still between the lathe centres. This will smarten things up.

SANDING
Take some 90 grit sandpaper and run a strip of masking tape down one side of the back of the sheet. Use scissors to cut off the strip and hold it against the leg (Fig. 18). Keep your hands clear of the turning, and never allow them to stray between the rest and the turning. Put on a dust mask and turn on the lathe.

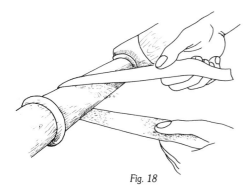

Fig. 18

Suddenly, the leg, with its gun barrel, beads and cove will look terrific.

Unless you feel you need more practice, you should start to turn the four legs of the stool.

PROBLEMS WITH TURNING

- If there is excessive vibration during initial turning, the leg is out of balance. Choose a slower speed or remove the corners of the leg between the top and bottom shoulders with an axe or large chisel before commencing turning.

- If the live centre slips and loses its grip on the turning, there is inadequate tailstock pressure or you are trying to remove too much wood too quickly.

- High-pitched screaming coming from the lathe suggests that the bearings, including the point of the tailstock, need oil.

- If the skew chisel bounces, leaving a smooth but irregular finish, your chisel is blunt, you are removing too much wood, you are exerting too much pressure on the turning or your grip on the chisel is too weak.

- If the beads are slashed by the skew chisel, you have moved the chisel too suddenly or poor lighting has led to clumsiness. Alternatively, you are not holding the chisel at right angles to the tool rest or you are not holding it tightly enough.

- If the gouge refuses to make a clean entry when you are cutting a cove, you are holding the tool at the wrong angle to the workpiece or the gouge is not twisted enough to allow the cutting edge of the lower side to cut into the wood.

Planing the legs

When you have turned and sanded all four legs, place each one in the vice and plane up the four ends. Choose two adjacent sides on each leg, and plane them square with each other, and also make sure they are straight by holding a straightedge along them. Each time you finish squaring up a pair of sides, mark them with the symbols denoting face side and face edge.

When all the legs have been squared up, group them in pairs.

Marking arrangements

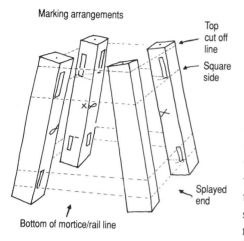

Top cut off line

Square side

Splayed end

Bottom of mortice/rail line

Fig. 19

Marking the joints in the legs

Fig. 19 shows the marking arrangements necessary for accurate jointing. Because the legs in the end elevation are splayed, the cutting lines at the top and bottom of the leg must also be cut at the same angle on that plane.

Lay the legs on the bench. Identify the outside faces of one pair. (These are the sides that are not squared and marked with the cross or loop.) Place these together, each with a squared face touching, and the other squared and marked face flat on the bench. Take the marking guide that you used for the turning, locate the top shoulder mark against the top shoulder of one of the legs and mark off the top of the leg with a pencil (Fig. 20).

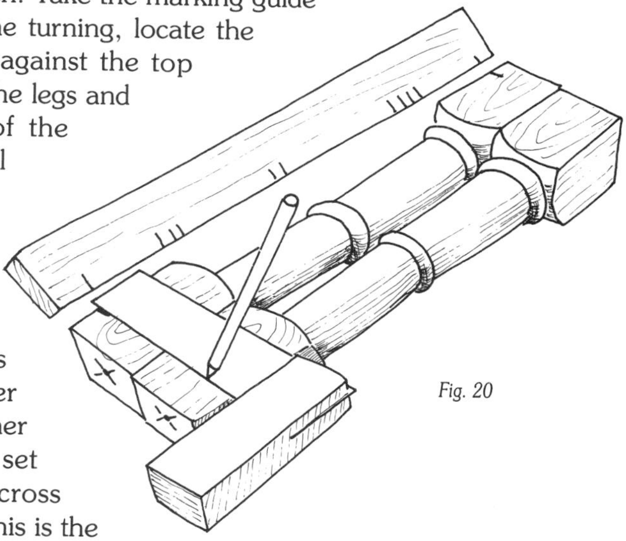

Fig. 20

Hold the two legs together and transfer this mark to the other leg. Then use a set square to square across the top of the leg. This is the cut-off line for the top of the leg, but its other plane is at an angle, and this is marked now.

Set your angle bevel to the angle at which the legs splay from the vertical. Lock the bevel in position. Set the bevel at each end of the pencil line you have just drawn and mark the upwards angle.

The top of the leg should look as illustrated in Fig. 21, with the line marked from the bevel rising above the cut-off line of the first mark into the waste at the end of the leg. When both splay lines have been drawn, join across on the inside with a set square. Repeat for the other three legs.

From now on, this cut-off line is your reference point for marking out the joints for the rails and for the stretchers beneath.

The mortices in these legs are ⅜in (9mm) wide and 3½in (88mm) long, and they are set down 1in (25mm) from the top of the leg. Set the points of the mortice gauge to the blade

Fig. 21

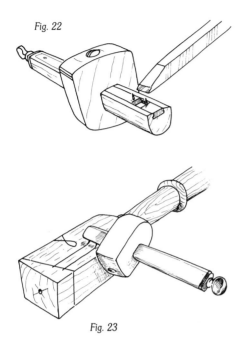

Fig. 22

Fig. 23

width of your ⅜in (9mm) chisel, or the nearest size to it (Fig. 22). In each leg the mortices are cut into the two adjacent sides that are marked square. The only known right angle then is the inside corner of each leg. The fence of the mortice gauge rests against an outside face and the lines are scribed on to the squared faces (Fig. 23).

Mark off all four mortices on each leg. The lower stretcher mortices are 2½in (65mm) long, and they share the same mortice gauge setting as the rail mortices. Mark the position for the lower mortices by using the marking guide.

Cutting a mortice

Place the leg horizontally in the vice, mortice facing up. Slide a scrap of timber under the leg to lift the face level with the bench and tighten the vice.

Take your mortice chisel and mallet and place the chisel a little way in from the end marks of the mortice. Hold it there and check that it is vertical in both planes. Now hit the top of the chisel with a mallet, giving it a good hard crack. The chisel will probably make a rather disappointing cut, no more than ⅛in (4mm) deep. Move the chisel back ⅛in (4mm) and make another cut. Rock the chisel a little, and in doing this you should remove the chip between them. Now move down the mortice by ¼in (6mm) and make another cut. Continue on down the mortice, stopping ¼in (6mm) before the chisel reaches the end.

This first row of cuts has to be precise. Each cut should be inside the scribe lines and vertical, and the chips should be small enough to break free easily (Fig. 24).

Fig. 24

Lever to clear waste

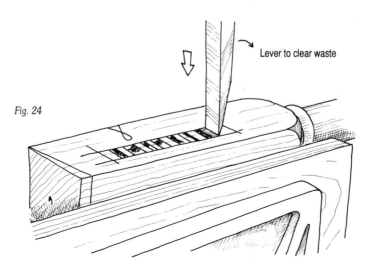

Now make the second row. Start in the first cut again and hit downwards hard. Move back about ⅜in (9mm) and, with the chisel leaning back slightly, give the chisel a couple of blows with the mallet. This should lift out a much bigger chip. Work down the mortice, taking as much out with each blow as you can. Remember to stop well clear of the ends of the mortice, and to keep clearing it, otherwise you will lose touch with the depth you have reached.

The mortices are all about 1¾in (45mm) deep. When you have cleaned out the bulk of the mortice, turn the chisel around and, holding it vertical, cut the remaining waste from the lower end of the mortice (Fig. 25). Remove the waste by levering the chisel against the top end of the mortice, before removing the waste at that end. Some rounding of the edge of the mortice is bound to occur at the top end, but this part is inside the joint and will not be seen. Repeat with all the long rail mortices.

At first, you can expect each mortice to take 15–20 minutes, but very soon you will speed up and should be able to complete a mortice of this length in 10 minutes at the most. The shorter (stretcher) mortices will take less time. Remember to keep the excavations tidy and their walls perpendicular.

Cutting the rails and stretchers

Cut the stretchers and rails roughly to length. When you lift the drawings from the plans, remember that you must allow 1½in (38mm) at each end for the tenons and that you must take account of the splay that makes the end rails and stretchers a little longer than you might expect. Plane these all smooth and remove most of the roughness on the inside surfaces as well. Plane the lower edges square and straight, and mark and plane the top edge to leave the rails 4½in (115mm) wide and the stretchers 2½in (65mm) wide.

Check that the angle bevel is still set to the same splay that was marked on the legs, and use it as a guide when you plane the top edges of the two long rails to the splay angle (Fig. 26).

Carving the rails

Each rail is carved with a simple strip of moulding along its centre and a bead along its lower edge. The moulding is done entirely by chisel, gouge and mallet, and is left marked by these tools (Fig. 27). A machine finish would be inappropriate.

To cut the main moulding down the centre of each rail I used a no. 10 veiner gouge and a no. 5 slightly curved gouge. The

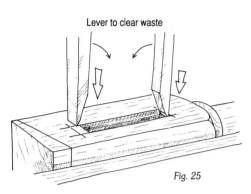

Lever to clear waste

Fig. 25

Fig. 26

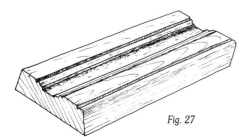

Fig. 27

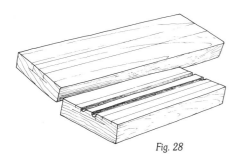

Fig. 28

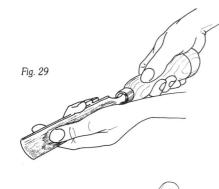

Fig. 29

Fig. 30

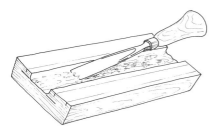

Fig. 31

edges were carved with the veiner, and the narrow groove cut with a V parting chisel. For the bead I used a 60 degree V parting chisel and a no. 8 gouge.

Draw in the sides of the parallel channel in the middle of the first rail with a ruler and a pencil or ball-point pen and at the ends mark off a depth line, a little over ¼in (6mm) deep (Fig. 28). Hold the rail tightly in the vice and use the veiner and mallet to remove the waste from inside the lines.

If you have not done much wood carving, the following tips might be helpful:

- Hold the gouge as shown in Fig. 29. Use your left hand to control the movement of the gouge. Your right hand, which grips the handle, supplies the necessary force, and twisting the handle with the thumb and first finger of your left hand adjusts the segment of the blade that makes the cut. This is useful when, for example, you are working into a confined space. If you are using a veiner you can twist the blade so that the sharpest curve of the blade cuts into the corner.

- Try to cut with the grain, across the grain or diagonally. Avoid having to cut against the grain, because the tool will be difficult to control and will leave a ragged cut.

- Start each cut deep and exit at a gentle angle.

- Each cut should remove its own shaving.

When you have roughly excavated the channel, use the veiner to remove the waste as deeply and closely as possible to the lines bordering the channel (Fig. 30).

Take the no. 8 gouge and, using a mallet, clean away the waste between the two lines. Then, without using the mallet, take the no. 5 gouge and smooth the floor of the channel (Fig. 31). Now pencil in the lines that mark the moulding. Use the V parting tool and mallet to cut the line that defines the outer edge of the moulding and the veiner to cut its sweep (Figs. 32 and 33).

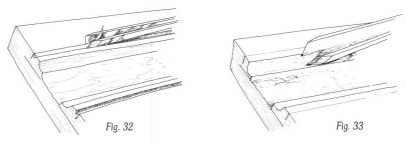

Fig. 32

Fig. 33

The bead at the bottom of the rail is cut next. First, use the V parting tool to cut the groove. Next, use a no. 8 gouge, held at a slight angle with its sharpening bevel upwards, to round off the corner (Fig. 34).

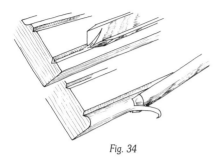

Fig. 34

Cutting the tenons

Cut the tenons on the front and back rails first. As you can see from the plans, their shoulders are at right angles, so marking out is straightforward.

Mark in the first shoulder 1½in (38mm) in from one end, and square around the rail using a knife and set square. Now mark off the length of the rail, which is 14in (356mm), for the second shoulder. Check your measurement and then square around the rail with the knife and set square. A pencil line 1½in (38mm) on will define the end of the rail, and any excess can be removed with a tenon saw.

Take the mortice gauge and adjust its fence measurement. The outside faces of the rails are not flush with the legs but are set in slightly, so if the gauge has not already been adjusted since you cut the mortices, the fence offset for the tenon cheeks will have to be reduced a little. See if you can set the fence so that, when you are cutting the face side of the tenon, the saw will take the thinnest possible sliver of wood from the base of the carved channel. For this the offset is likely to be a little less than ⅜in (9mm) (Fig. 35).

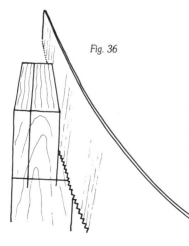

Fig. 35

Fig. 36

Mark around the end of the rail, pressing the fence of the mortice gauge against the face side and continuing the marks down the rail edges to the shoulder-lines. Because of the channel, you will find it difficult to mark the middle part of the tenon on the end. Leave this, and join the marks that are there with a ruler and ball-point pen, which is better than a scribe line, because the ink line is easier to see.

Hold the rail in the vice, tilted at an angle away from where you are standing. From your viewpoint, which is above and in line with the vice, you should be able to see both lines running to the shoulder and their continuation across the end of the rail. When you use a hand saw, it is a little difficult to know how to find the best viewpoint from which to control the blade. Obviously, you have to stand sideways to the bench and face the side of the rail in the vice as it leans away from you. When you drop the saw into position on the top corner of the rail, on the waste side of the cheek line (closest to the bench), the saw will divide your view. Lean your head a little to the left and watch from there (Fig. 36). Your view will

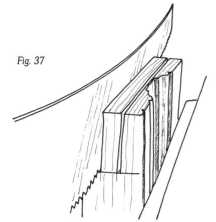

Fig. 37

show the blade, the scribe line to which it is cutting and the top of the rail. It does not show what you are cutting off.

The second line to saw will be the cheek cut further from the bench. This time, tilt your head to the right to watch the blade from the bench side. Again, you will have a clear view of the tenon and the scribe line (Fig. 37).

Tighten the vice. Take a large, sharp rip saw and start the saw cut on the waste side of the line. Do not press, and watch the tip of the saw as it begins its progress into the end of the rail. When the saw has reached the shoulder nearest you, the saw will barely have reached to the centre of the rail (Fig. 38).

Turn the rail around and repeat on the opposite edge, correcting any deviance of the blade in the centre of the rail. To do this you have to lift the saw handle a little this time. Your second cut should continue until the tip of the blade has reached the first saw cut you made (Fig. 39).

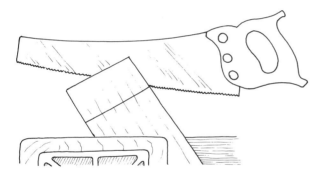

Fig. 38

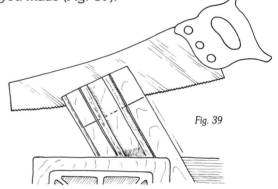

Fig. 39

Slacken the vice and pull the rail vertical. Hold the saw horizontal and complete the first cut. Stop the saw when it reaches the shoulder-line (Fig. 40).

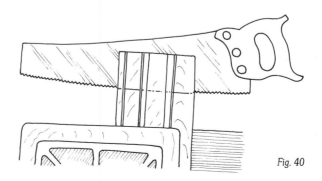

Fig. 40

Repeat on the face side of the tenon, and then saw the tenons at the other end of the rail. Saw the sides of the tenons of the opposite rail in the same way.

REMOVING THE WASTE

Place the rail horizontally in the vice, face side downwards, with the tenon just clear of the jaws. Take a sharp chisel and cut a fine slither of wood from the waste side of the tenon's shoulder. Because the shoulder-line was originally scribed with a knife, this cross-grain slither should come free readily and leave a well-defined shallow channel on the waste side of the shoulder-line (Fig. 41).

Rest the tenon saw in this channel and draw it back and forth a few times, pressing downwards quite firmly. Once the cut is established, saw off the waste. With a little practice, you will be able to make perfectly clean-cut shoulders that need no further trimming. Repeat on the opposite side and at the other tenons.

The tenons that are cut in the short splayed ends are sawn in the same way, but a little more care is required in marking them, and both the set square and angle bevel should be used to mark the shoulders (Fig. 42).

Once the tenon is sawn, it will have to be trimmed away on its underside to fit in the mortice. Place the end in the vice and use a flat chisel and mallet to chop away the lower corner of the tenon until the shoulder and the cut you have just made form a right angle (Fig. 43).

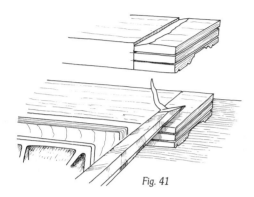

Fig. 41

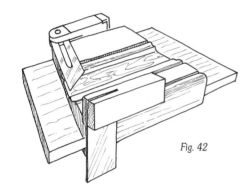

Fig. 42

Fig. 43

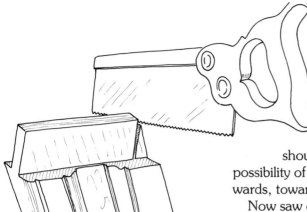

The top of each tenon will also have to be trimmed. The mortices all stop short 1in (25mm) from the top of the leg. Take each rail in turn and saw downwards and at right angles to the tenon shoulders until the tip of the saw touches the shoulder on the back of the rail. It should not mark the front shoulder, and to avoid any possibility of this happening, you should tilt the saw point downwards, towards the back of the rail as you are using it (Fig. 44).

Now saw off the waste, again missing the front shoulder, and trim back any that remains to the line with a chisel and mallet.

You will notice in the plans that the inside corner of each tenon is mitred. This is so that adjacent tenons do not obstruct each other as they are pulled into the leg. Place each rail in turn in the vice, tilting it so that the tenon is clear of the top of the bench. Mark the mitre free-hand, then saw it using a panel saw or a large tenon saw (Fig. 45).

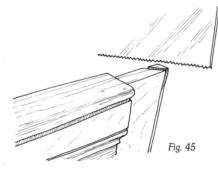

Fig. 44

Fitting the tenons

Fit the front and back rails first. Number the tenons and the mortices to avoid confusion, and then place the legs in the vice one at a time and fit the appropriate tenon. Some will be rather loose; others too tight. There is not much you can do to remedy a loose tenon, except to remember to slot a thin slice of wood against the tenon to pack out the joint when you are gluing the stool together. If the joint is too tight, check first that the mortice is cut to the correct size. A quick inspection of the mortice will tell you whether the overall size is right, and if it is not, it is a moment's work to chop it to size with a morticing chisel. If the length and width are correct, check to see if the sides are vertical. Do this by slipping a ⅜in (9mm) mortice chisel into the mortice and sight down the leg. The chisel should stand vertically in the mortice when the leg is resting on the bench. If the mortice is cut at an angle, correct the angle using a sharp bevel-edged chisel (Fig. 46).

If it is the tenon that is too large, inspect it carefully. There will not be many marks to guide you, so first test that the face side of the tenon is set back from the face side of the rail by the correct amount. Do this by placing the rail face side down on the bench, and slip a strip of wood the width of the offset beneath the tenon. If it does not fit, remove a few shavings from the face side of the tenon with a shoulder plane or chisel (Fig. 47). If the tenon still does not fit, tentatively remove a couple of

Fig. 45

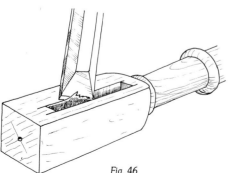

Fig. 46

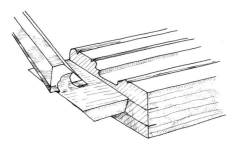

Fig. 47

shavings from the back face of the tenon. Check after every couple of shavings, until the tenon slides stiffly into place.

When all the joints are fitted, try fitting adjacent tenons. If there is any difficulty in fitting two into one leg, you have either tried to push a tenon into the wrong mortice or the two tenons are touching as they meet in the middle of the leg. If you withdraw one tenon and inspect its end, you will usually see bruise marks on the tenon where it has rubbed. The fault is that the mitres are not at 45 degrees, and they can be corrected with a shoulder plane or chisel.

Making the stretchers

The stretchers are 2½in (65mm) wide and about 1in (25mm) thick. You will need two that are 17in (432mm) long and two 11½in (292mm) long. Plane them to size, and mark the face side and face edge of each one. Mark the tenon shoulders of the front and back stretchers (these are 14in (356mm) apart, the same as the rails) and saw the tenons.

Mark the tenon shoulders of the end stretchers. This dimension can be lifted directly from the drawings, but it might be worth assembling the end rails and legs and measuring the length exactly (Fig. 48). If there is more than a ⅛in (4mm) discrepancy between the two pairs of legs, you will need to adjust one of the rail shoulders before deciding on the length of the stretcher.

Fig. 48

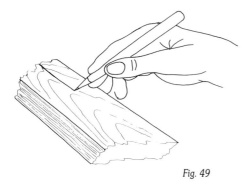

Fig. 49

When you are marking the end stretchers, remember to use the angle bevel to splay the tenon shoulders. Saw the tenons.

The stretchers have a very simple moulding worked along the top, and a bead moulding on their bottom edges.

Pencil the lines for the V-cut for the bead and for the top moulding free-hand. If you hold the pencil as shown in Fig. 49, using the second, third and fourth fingers as a fence to control the pencil, you will find this a quick and accurate way of drawing parallel lines close to the edge of a board.

There is one line on the inside of each rail and two on the outside. There is no need to carve a bead on the inside. Cut along the lines with the V parting chisel, controlling its progress and depth of cut with the left hand and hitting it with the mallet held in the right. Now use the no. 5 sweep gouge, held with the bevel upwards, to cut the radius at the top of the rail. Repeat on the inside, and then cut the bead at the bottom of the rail, using a no. 8 gouge.

ASSEMBLY

The stool is assembled in three stages: the splayed ends first, then the tops and bottoms of the legs are trimmed. The front and back rails and stretchers are then glued in, and, when the framework has been levelled, the top is joined, carved and pegged to the framework.

Pegged mortices

The mortice joints are all glued and pegged. The pegs are used to draw the joints together and so clamps are not needed (Fig. 50).

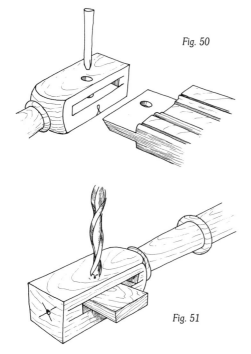

Fig. 50

Fig. 51

Split some straight-grained oak strips a little more than ¼in (6mm) square. Take each in turn and hold it against the bench hook. Carve them into pegs, slightly tapered, with a point at the end. You will need two pegs for each rail mortice and one for each stretcher mortice.

Fit a ¼in (6mm) drill bit in the electric drill. Position the drill as illustrated in Fig. 51 and drill right through the mortice and out through the inside of the leg. To avoid splintering the inside of the mortice, slip a tight fitting scrap of waste wood into it before drilling. Repeat with the other mortices.

Now press the tenon into the joint. Tap it in as hard as you can and lay the assembly flat. If you peer into the drill hole you

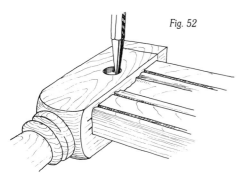

Fig. 52

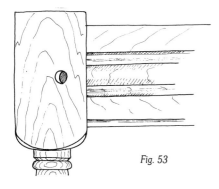

Fig. 53

will see the tenon blocking your view through the leg. Take a centre-punch and position it against the side of the hole and tap it with a hammer (Fig. 52).

Dismantle the two pieces. Lay the tenon on a piece of waste wood to stop it rocking and drill through the tenon, using the centre-punch mark as your centre. Assemble the joint again, and you will see that the two holes are misaligned (Fig. 53). When it is driven in, the peg will draw the joint together.

Drill the other tenons in a similar manner.

Gluing

The mortice joints are glued as well as pegged. White PVA glue is suitable and so is animal glue. Whichever glue you use, try to keep adhesive away from the finished surfaces. This stool has a waxed finish, but it is stained before waxing, and any glue that is left on the wood will repel the stain and make it difficult to obtain an even colour.

Apply the glue to the inside top edge of each mortice. The tenon will spread the glue as it is pressed in and very little will squeeze out at the shoulders.

If some glue does spill on the work, wash it away with a brush and copious amounts of cold clean water.

Trimming the ends

Once the pair of splayed legs is pegged to the rails and stretchers and the glue has dried, take each pair of legs in turn, and with your straightedge aligned with the top of the rail, mark across the tops of the legs (Fig. 54). Square around the sides of the legs with a set square, and saw off the waste above the lines with a tenon saw.

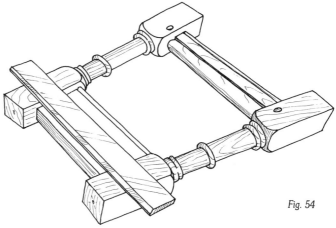

Fig. 54

Now fit the front and back rails. Check that they line up with the top of the legs. Increase the lengths of the mortices until they do.

Fit the stretchers and assemble the stool framework. When each joint is checked, drill and peg the joints.

The top

The top is made from two pieces of oak glued together and held with three concealed tenons (Fig. 55). Choose interesting pieces of wood for the top, with knots, burrs and figure. A board with an interesting grain pattern is unlikely to be flat when you find it and is not likely to remain flat after you have planed it, but it will look the best.

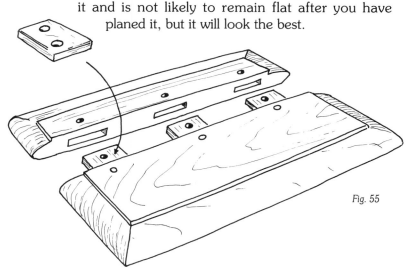

Fig. 55

Join enough pieces to make the 14in (356mm) width required and plane the joining faces. (For advice on shooting joints see pages 11 and 151.) Assemble the boards and mark on the top faces the positions for the three concealed tenons.

Square across the edges of the top planks and complete the marking of the mortices with the mortice gauge. Chop out the mortices to a depth of little more than 1in (25mm). (For advice on morticing by hand, see page 38, with a router, see page 55.)

Saw out some straight-grained, loose tenons, trim the ends so that they are easy to drive into the mortices and cut them to length to suit the depth of mortices in the top. Glue and peg the tenons into one plank (Fig. 56). While you are still holding the drill, drill through the mortices in the other plank before you use draw pegs to hold the joint.

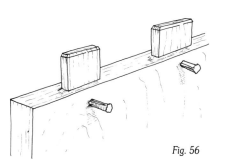

Fig. 56

Fit the planks together, tap them until they fit tightly and centre-punch the tenons as described above. Separate the planks and drill the tenons.

Glue and peg the two pieces together.

Planing the top

Smoothing a plank with a turbulent grain such as this is going to be awkward. First, sharpen your plane (see page 153), set the blade to its finest cut and rub some candle wax on its sole.

Clamp the board to the bench or rest it against a bench stop, and experiment to find which direction you can best plane it. As long as your plane iron is set to its meanest setting, you will eventually find a direction that copes with the confused grain. To begin with, try planing at right angles or at 45 degrees to the grain.

When you have subdued the top, turn over the plank and roughly smooth the underside. This will not be seen and so does not need to be smooth, but you might as well remove the marks and roughness left by modern machines.

Carving the moulding

There is a simple moulding carved into the edge of the top. Pencil a line around the edge and two-thirds down from the top. Next pencil in a line around the perimeter of the top, a little over 1in (25mm) in from the edge (Fig. 57).

Clamp the top to the bench. Use a mallet and the veiner gouge to carve a groove, ³⁄₁₆in (5mm) deep, right around the perimeter of the top, next to the line. Hold the gouge at the angle illustrated in Fig. 58.

Take the no. 5 gouge and carve away the waste from the edge of the top until the moulding resembles Fig. 59. Turn the gouge over to smooth the work.

Place the top on edge in the vice, and plane a bevel on the underside.

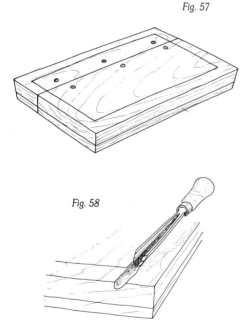

Fig. 57

Fig. 58

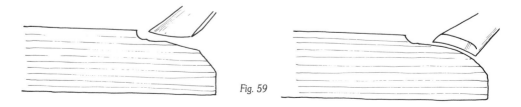

Fig. 59

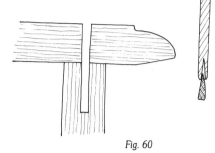
Fig. 60

Fixing the top

The top is pegged to the base. Clamp the top in position. Either by sighting or measuring, mark a centre mark for a peg, which should go into the appropriate leg. Drill a hole for each peg with a ¼in (6mm) drill bit, and make a selection of pegs of the right size to drive into the holes. Dip their points in glue before hammering them into the stool. You can split the points of some of the pegs and insert wedges in the split before you hammer the pegs home (Fig. 60). These will be very strong.

After the corners are pegged, remove the clamps and drill holes through the top into the rails. Drive pegs into these holes as well.

Trim the pegs with a loose hack saw blade. You can protect the surface of the top by slipping a sheet of card with a hole in the middle over the pegs that need trimming, and then rest the saw blade on the card (Fig. 61). Finish trimming with a chisel.

Fig. 61

FINISHING

Faking an antique effect

The stool in the photograph is made of oak. We wanted to give it an 'antiqued' look, although we stopped short of distressing the wood and drilling woodworm holes.

The stool has a mottled black-brown colour. It is quite easy to apply a flat stain or to fume a piece evenly, but old oak furniture is mottled, and this effect is difficult to reproduce. When we started, the stool was the colour of fresh straw – a pale golden-yellow colour. The first thing we did was to brush a copious coating of dilute tannic acid all over the stool and let it soak in. Oak has tannic acid in it anyway and will turn dark when it is exposed to ammonia gas, but by adding tannic acid, you can achieve a deeper colour and the process is a little quicker.

To get the mottled effect, we had to mask off parts of the stool, particularly the outer surfaces of the legs, areas of the top and parts of the lower rail, which would normally be bleached by the sun. We achieved this by squirting large quantities of tomato ketchup on to the stool, and then dabbing and spreading it around with a dry rag. We then enclosed the stool in a large plastic bin liner and, before sealing the top, placed a dish of ammonia on the floor between the legs of the stool. We closed the top and left the stool to fume for about 5 hours. Every hour or so, we re-arranged the bag to ensure that the gas circulated and reached every part.

Warning

Cabinet-makers' suppliers sell ammonia gas dissolved in water. When you decant a little of the fluid into a dish it immediately gives off a pungent, choking gas. Do not inhale the gas or let its fumes reach your eyes. When you pour out the ammonia and take it to the bag in which you have placed the stool, make the distances you travel as short as possible and work quickly, holding your breath. After the piece has been fumed, open the bag in a well-ventilated area and hold your breath.

Colouring the stool

Wash the stool with a stiff brush and clean water and leave it to dry. When it is dry, the stool will be a little paler. If you need to add colour to darken areas or to break up some of the more effectively masked areas, you can stain it with a Colron oil stain. For more localized colouring and antiquing, mix some dry colours – brown umber and a little black – with some white PVA glue and a little water, and dab the mixture where you need the colour. The colours will dry, leaving a white residue of glue on the surface. Make sure the stool is completely dry before burnishing all its surfaces with a cotton cloth until it is smooth and slightly shiny.

Waxing

Apply plenty of coats of soft brown wax. Leave time between each coat for the wax to dry and continue to build up the wax finish. The more soft furniture wax that is applied, the better the stool will look. Once you have applied soft, slow-drying wax, you should never rub on a quick-drying wax, because the solvents are different and will strip off the earlier finish.

SIDE TABLE

This is a copy of a French provincial side table. It is simple and elegant, only 22in (about 560mm) wide and 45in (1145mm) long, but it is large enough to be drawn out and used as a small dining table when required. The legs are a little unusual in that they are shaped in only one plane, which makes them easy to cut out with an electric jig saw.

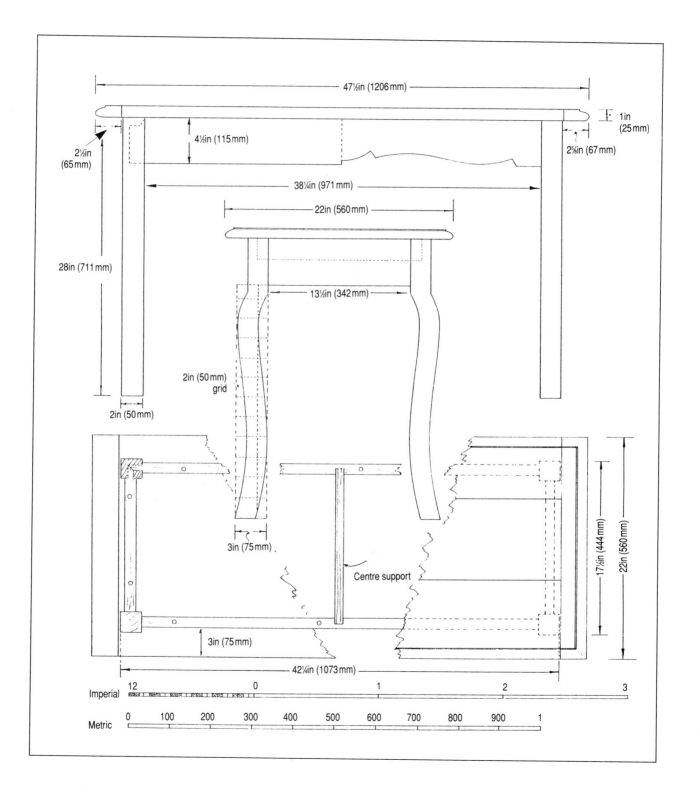

47½in (1206mm)

1in (25mm)

4½in (115mm)

2⅝in (67mm)

2½in (65mm)

38¼in (971mm)

22in (560mm)

28in (711mm)

13½in (342mm)

2in (50mm) grid

2in (50mm)

3in (75mm)

Centre support

17½in (444mm)

22in (560mm)

3in (75mm)

42¼in (1073mm)

Imperial   12   0   1   2   3

Metric   0   100   200   300   400   500   600   700   800   900   1

CONSTRUCTION

The table in the illustration is made from lime wood, although the original on which it is based was made from fruit wood. You could use almost any solid timber, or you could combine different woods. I made this one in about 20 hours, which included a morning spent sawing the wood into planks and planing them smooth.

The legs are cut from solid planks, 2in (50cm) thick and 3in (75mm) wide. The base framework is made from planks measuring 4½ × 1in (115 × 25mm) and is morticed together with mortices that are ½in (12mm) wide and 1½in (38mm) deep.

The top is made of planks, glued together edge to edge. I cut a groove in each jointed edge and inserted a loose tongue to hold the planks level while they were gluing. This is not necessary and does not strengthen the joint, but it is quick and easy to do it if you have a biscuit jointer or router. If the planks are prevented from sliding around while they are being clamped, planing and sanding smooth after the glue has dried is kept to a minimum.

Narrow cleats are fitted at each end of the table top. These are also held with loose tongues, 1½in (38mm) wide, and then glued. The grooves are stopped short at the end of each cleat, so they are not visible from the sides. Across the centre of the base framework is a strut measuring 1 × 2in (25 × 50mm) to support the table top (Fig. 1).

The top is held to the framework with wooden pegs. In addition, eight short, heavy woodscrews are recessed inside the framework, and secure the top from below.

Fig. 1

The legs

Sort your planks into groups. Keep the top planks to one side and start with the legs.

You will need to make a card or hardboard template in order to mark out the legs. The squared drawing on the plans will help you to draw it. The drawing is to scale and the squares represent 2in (50mm) square. Reproduce the grid full size on a scrap of hardboard. Mark on your grid lines the points at which the lines of the leg intersect the grid. Join the lines free-hand or use some curves cut from a strip of cardboard to help and you will have an accurate, full-sized outline of the legs.

MORTICING THE LEGS

It is much easier to clamp the legs if you mortice them before cutting them to shape.

On each leg, find two adjacent faces that are at right angles to each other and mark them with the face side and face edge symbols. From the leg template, mark in the top and bottom of the leg, and, using the top line, measure down 4½in (115mm) to give the line for the bottom of the mortice. Mark up 3¾in (95mm) to give the top of the mortice. Square these marks around to the face edge (Fig. 2). Repeat on the other legs.

The mortices are ½in (12mm) wide, and set in from the outside of the leg by ½in (12mm) and from the inside by 1in (25mm). Set the mortice gauge points to ½in (12mm) and the fence to 1in (25mm), and scribe in the mortices (Fig. 3).

If you are going to rout the mortices, you need only mark up the first mortice you cut, but if you are going to chop out the mortices by hand, you must scribe all eight. (For instructions on cutting mortices with a mallet and chisel see pages 37–9.)

ROUTING MORTICES

I use a Bosch POF 50 router, which has a powerful motor and a plunge mechanism. If your router does not have a plunge facility, you will have to mount it in a drill press and arrange a fence. It generally takes me a little longer to mortice using the press.

Fit a long, ½in (12mm), two-flute cutter in the router and tighten the collet. Grip the top of the leg in the vice, with the marks of the first mortice facing upwards. Place the router on the leg. By adjusting the fence, position the router bit until it is between the mortice scribe lines (Fig. 4). Tighten the fence and adjust the plunge depth stop to 1½in (38mm). Wear safety spectacles and ear muffs.

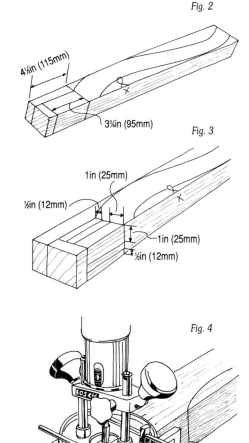

Fig. 2

4½in (115mm)

3¾in (95mm)

Fig. 3

1in (25mm)

½in (12mm)

1in (25mm)

½in (12mm)

Fig. 4

The quickest way I have found to rout deep mortices is to start at one end and plunge the router to full depth. Withdraw the router bit, move the router along half the diameter of the hole you have just bored and plunge again.

The problem to begin with is to get the router bit to reach full depth. If you try plunging straight downwards you are likely to burn the wood and overheat the bit. To avoid this you have to start the mortice with a series of small plunges, working up and down at the top end of the mortice, deepening the hole in small steps. It will take only three or four such steps to enable the router to reach 1½in (38mm), and then the rest of the mortice can be completed rapidly (Fig. 5).

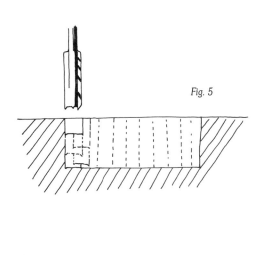

Fig. 5

When you have finished routing the first mortice, turn the leg around and plunge out the adjacent mortice, which will meet the one you have just finished in the centre of the leg. Knock out the waste from both mortices. Turn to the other legs and finish the mortices on those.

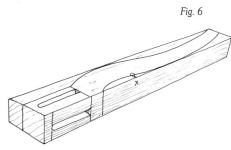

Fig. 6

SHAPING THE LEGS

Take the template and lay it in position on the leg. Check that the end marks line up and then pencil around the template (Fig. 6).

Place the leg in the vice, and clamp it very tightly. Fit a large-toothed (T111c) blade in the jig saw and, starting at the bottom of the leg, cut towards the top.

Hold the jig saw as illustrated (Fig. 7). The right hand controls the on/off switch (and, on the Bosch jig saw, the speed of the motor) and also exerts pressure to keep the bed of the saw tight against the leg. Tuck your left hand on to the body of the motor at the back. The left hand steers the saw and exerts a forward momentum. Always keep your hands away from the front of the saw, and make sure that your fingers and the electric power cable are kept well clear of the blade.

Set the orbital action to maximum and saw up the outside of the leg. If you use a sharp blade, it will take very little time to make the cut and the finish should be smooth. Give the saw only the slightest forward pressure: the orbital action tends to pull the blade into the wood, and for most sawing action that is about all the help the saw will need. Excessive forward pressure will cause the tip of the blade to wander.

Fig. 7

Finish the remaining cuts. The last ones are the straight cut at the top of the leg and the curved cut to meet it. As you finish the straight cut, change the orbital setting to zero, and do the same at the end of the curved cut. If you do not do this, the tip of

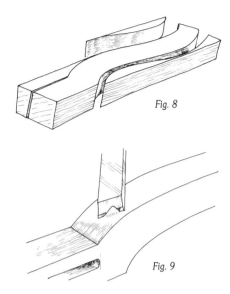

Fig. 8

Fig. 9

the blade will progress a little too far and spoil your work (Fig. 8).

Cut out all the legs, then take one leg at a time. Shave away any bumps and roughness with a 1½in (38mm) chisel, held with the sharpening bevel facing upwards (Fig. 9).

When you have done this, use a spokeshave to smooth the long curves of the lower leg. Finish with a cabinet scraper. (For advice on using a spokeshave and a cabinet scraper see pages 152 and 154–5.)

Before you finish with the legs, place the top of the leg in the vice, take a ½in (12mm) chisel and chop the ends of the mortice square with a chisel.

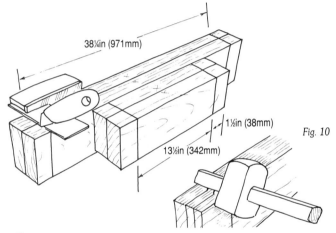

38¼in (971mm)

1½in (38mm)

13½in (342mm)

Fig. 10

The rails

Saw the rails to width and length, and plane the two edges and the outside face smooth.

Mark off the shoulders for the tenons (Fig. 10) and use the marking gauge to scribe the tenons. Cut the sides of the tenons with a rip saw and remove the waste on each side with a tenon saw (see pages 41–3). Trim the tops of the tenons and mitre their ends to fit into the mortices.

Align the two long side rails and clamp them together in the vice, top edge upmost. Take the support strut and put it across the two rails. Mark its width on the top edges with a knife.

Separate the two rails. Taking one at a time, square across the top of the rail and down the inside. Set a marking gauge to ⅜in (9mm) and scribe a line across these lines to mark the end of the slot for the strut. Repeat on the other rail and then change the marking gauge setting to 2in (50mm) and mark the depth of both slots (Fig. 12).

Fig. 11

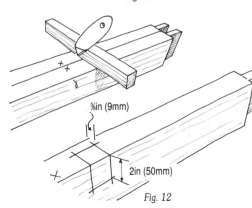

⅜in (9mm)

2in (50mm)

Fig. 12

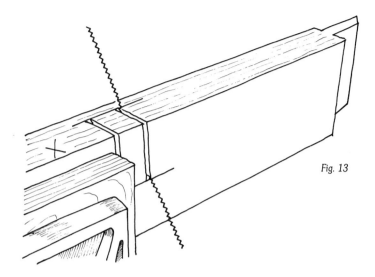

Fig. 13

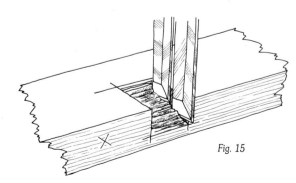

Fig. 14

The slots are cut as follows. Hold the rail in the vice and use a tenon saw to cut down the sides of the slot. Stop when your saw reaches the scribe line (Fig. 13). Select a sharp bevel-edged chisel, ½–¾in (12–20mm) wide, and use this to chop out the waste between the saw cuts (Fig. 14).

Take the rail, place it face down on a smooth board and clamp it to the bench. Now hit the chisel vertically with a mallet, keeping it at right angles to the grain to weaken the wood between the saw cuts (Fig. 15). Remove the wood you have weakened and, still using the chisel, trim the sides and bottom of the slot square. Adjust its size until the strut fits (Fig. 16). It does not matter if, after all this, it is a trifle loose, because the joint cannot be seen, but the slot on the opposite rail can be a little tighter.

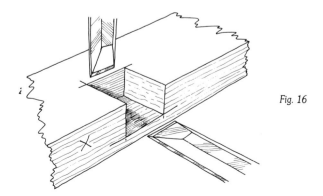

Fig. 16

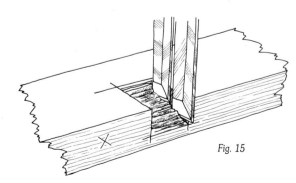

Fig. 15

A simple frieze is sawn into the bottom edge of the front rail. Pencil this in free-hand or use the grid on the plans to scale up the frieze. Saw it out using the jig saw. Remember that when you are using a jig saw and are sawing towards another saw cut, as the two cuts draw closer, you should reduce and then cancel the orbital cutting action. This will make a neater saw cut. If necessary, smooth the bottom edge of the rail with a file.

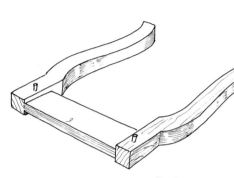

Fig. 17

ASSEMBLY

The joints are pegged and glued together. If you have a furniture clamp, you can immediately run glue into the mortices for the short end rail, insert the tenons into a pair of legs and clamp the joint tight. While the joint is still uncured, drill a couple of ⅜in (9mm) holes through each mortice and drive in a couple of pegs to hold the joint. You can then release the furniture clamp and use it for the pair at the other end. If you do not have a clamp long enough for this, you can draw the joints together with long, tapered pegs (Fig. 17), and instructions for doing this are on pages 46–7.

The top

The top of the table featured here is made from two wide planks with a slightly narrower plank fitted at the back to make up the width. It does not matter how many planks you use, but try to keep them all over 4in (100mm) wide, because it will look better. The ends of the boards are clamped by cleats, each held in position by a loose tongue.

Choose the boards for the top – they need to be 42½in (1080mm) long and 1in (25mm) thick. Lay them on the bench in the order in which you want to glue them. Number the joining edges so that you can work on matching pairs.

I used an electric jointer for shooting the joints between the planks. These are very useful tools, and they save a lot of time and labour. Bosch manufactures a bench-mounted attachment, which is fitted to an electric planer. This is a low-cost and satisfactory alternative to a purpose-made tool.

When you are using a jointer, apply downward pressure to the leading end of the board you are shooting, as you feed it into the cutter. Once you have passed approximately 12in (300mm) of wood over the blades, re-arrange your grip and press down

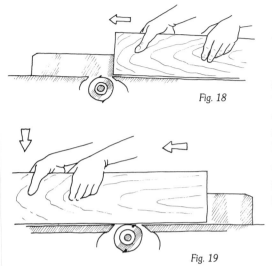

Fig. 18

Fig. 19

on the exit side (Figs. 18 and 19). (Instructions on shooting joints with a hand plane are on pages 11 and 151.

The jointing edges are grooved to accept a loose tongue. I have a biscuit jointer, which is an ideal tool for making stopped grooves, rebates and so on, and using it is simplicity itself. Set the blade to ¼in (6mm) depth and the fence to half the thickness of the plank. Then, holding the saw as illustrated in Fig. 20, start the motor and plunge the saw blade into the edge of the board. Push the tool along, keeping the fence pressed tight against the board. The small diameter circular blade cuts a groove ⅛in (4mm) wide, which is about the width of groove you need.

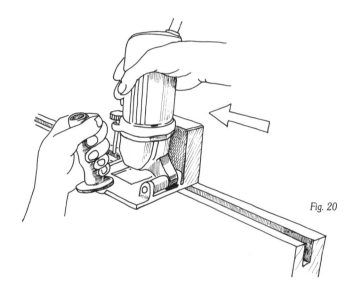

Fig. 20

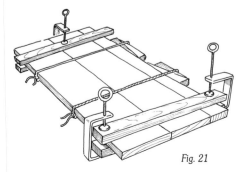

Fig. 21

If you do not have a biscuit jointer, you can lower the blade of your bench saw and run the plank on edge over the blade. Alternatively, you can cut the groove with a router.

Saw some strips of wood or hardboard to slip into the grooves and then glue and clamp the top together. If you have not got any sash cramps, you can use string and wedges instead (Fig. 21). Before you apply clamping pressure, make sure that the planks are prevented from buckling by sandwiching them between a pair of battens clamped at each end.

When the glue is dry, trim the ends square with a saw. Then plane the ends straight and square, working inwards from the edges. If you are using an electric plane, set the cutter to a mini-

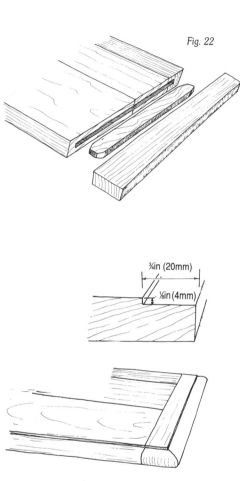

Fig. 22

¾in (20mm)

⅛in (4mm)

Fig. 23

mum cut and, with the fence pressed against the top surface of the table, plane it square in single, fine passes.

Plane up the cleats and leave them a little longer than the table width. Cut a ¾in (20mm) deep stopped groove in one edge of each cleat and at each end of the table, resting your fence against the top surface of the planks (Fig. 22). Cut a couple of loose tongues 1½in (38mm) wide and ⅛in (4mm) thick to insert into the grooves, and glue and clamp them in position. Stopping the grooves short of the edge of the table conceals the tongue and leaves a neat finish.

Before shaping the edge moulding, sand or plane the table top smooth. There will be a little sanding necessary later, but it is easier to use a rebate plane or router on the edge moulding if the top is smoothed. Saw off the waste from the ends of the cleats and plane around the sides of the table until they are straight and square with the top.

Cutting the edge moulding

The moulding I have used around the edge of this table is a little deeper and more oval in section than can be cut by a normal rounding over router cutter. The moulding was formed in two stages.

First, with a rebate plane or a router, cut a rebate around the edge of the table, ¾in (20mm) wide and ⅛in (4mm) deep (Fig. 23). From here it was an easy matter to round off the moulding with a rebate plane, used free-hand.

To start, hold the rebate plane with the second, third and little fingers of your right hand trailing behind the blade and controlling the plane's orientation as a fence would (Fig. 24). Work a bevel in the edge of the table, about ½in (12mm) wide and 45 degrees to the top and side edges.

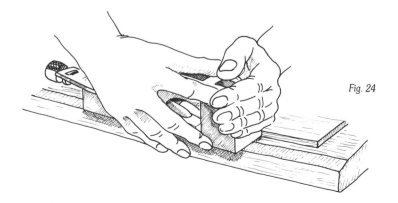

Fig. 24

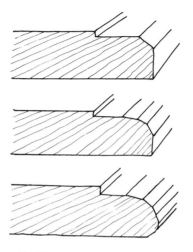

Fig. 25

When you have a regular bevel all the way round, change the position of the plane so that it removes the two sharp edges of the bevel. This effectively rounds the lip at the edge of the table, and from now on all you have to do is plane away sharp edges. Before very long the moulding will seem almost finished (Fig. 25).

From here, the moulding can be smoothed off with sandpaper, supported by a shaped block that echoes the curved lip of the moulding. It will speed things up if you can use a curved scraper to round off the edges. You can easily make a scraper from a scrap of silver steel. (Instructions for making and using moulding scrapers can be found on page 154.)

After rounding the edges and scraping the top, finish the preparation by sanding all the surfaces with 240 open cut sandpaper.

FINISHING

Lime wood is a white, even-textured and fairly featureless wood. After sanding, we stained the table with Colron stains, mixed to give the golden glow of finished cherry wood.

We added a very small amount of American Walnut stain to a pot of Canadian Cedar. The American Walnut is quite a deep, rich brown, and you need only a very small quantity to give substance to the orange cedar stain. We applied the mixture with a rag, working along the grain of the top planks and at right angles along the cleats. Before replenishing the rag we wiped the end-grain of the cleats. If a fully charged rag is used here, the end-grain will soak up more stain than is desirable. The rails were wiped with a wet rag, and the legs stained briskly, again before the rag was re-charged. This is because the end-grain in the curved legs would otherwise have drawn in too much stain and left them looking blotchy.

After leaving the table for 10 minutes, we followed with a dilute coat of garnet shellac. This is a deep greeny-brown polish, which, as it is applied, kills off the bright orange of the stain. Four thick coats were applied to the top, and three coats to the legs and rails. It is quite difficult to lay a smooth brush coat of shellac. Shellac dries very quickly, and brush marks and ridges of piled polish remain hardened on the surface. The finish will, in any case, be rubbed down with wire wool, which will take off the edges and remove most of the worst lumps on the finish.

However, if you can apply an even finish by brush, you will have less difficulty rubbing the surface down to a good finish.

To get the best finish, it is probably best to apply the shellac with a 3in (75mm) brush in the following manner. Shake the shellac thoroughly. Decant about a cupful into an open-topped dish. Dip the tips of the brush hairs into the shellac and wipe them against the edge of the dish to remove any excess. Start brushing the shellac on to the table about 3in (75mm) in from one end, and brush the shellac out towards the end of the table. Then bring the brush to where you began, and brush along towards the other end. Within about a minute, your brush will have run out. By now you should have applied shellac to a rectangle of wood, about 15in (380mm) long and 6in (150mm) wide. Recharge the brush, drain it against the dish edge and begin again, 3–4in (75–100mm) from where you finished, working back to where you left off, and then onwards towards the far end (Fig. 26).

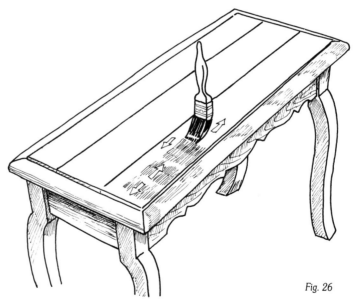

Fig. 26

Continue in this way. Do not try brushing fresh shellac on to polish that is still damp. Do not try to brush out irregularities, and try to avoid piling too much on too quickly. Leave the table top to dry for about 30 minutes before applying the next coat.

After leaving the table a few days for the shellac to harden, we rubbed it down with 000 wire wool and waxed it with black, quick-drying wax.

SCANDINAVIAN
ARMCHAIR

This is a noble chair, made almost entirely from pine. From the photograph you can see that the tenons of the backrest penetrate right through the back legs. With the single exception of the joints between the armrests and the back legs, all the joints are at right angles to each other, which makes marking out and cutting the joints straightforward.

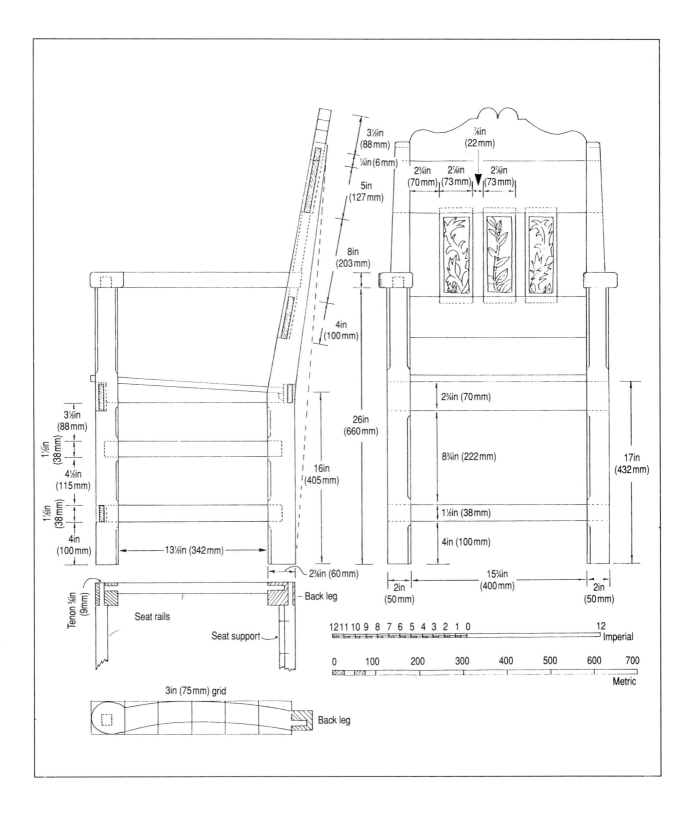

3½in (88mm)

¼in (6mm)

5in (127mm)

8in (203mm)

4in (100mm)

26in (660mm)

16in (405mm)

2⅜in (60mm)

⅞in (22mm)

2¾in (70mm)

2⅞in (73mm)

2⅞in (73mm)

2¾in (70mm)

8¾in (222mm)

1½in (38mm)

4in (100mm)

17in (432mm)

3½in (88mm)

1½in (38mm)

4½in (115mm)

1½in (38mm)

4in (100mm)

13½in (342mm)

2in (50mm)

15¾in (400mm)

2in (50mm)

Tenon ⅜in (9mm)

Seat rails

Seat support

Back leg

Back leg

3in (75mm) grid

12 11 10 9 8 7 6 5 4 3 2 1 0   12
Imperial

0   100   200   300   400   500   600   700
Metric

Pine is easy to obtain and easy to work with. The legs are made from 2in (50mm) thick floor joist, and the rails and backrests from planks that are a little over 1in (25mm) thick. The curved back legs were sawn using a Bosch jig saw, the rails and front legs were sawn on the table saw, and all the legs can be morticed using a router. The bulk of the construction work on this chair was completed in a little more than 10 hours. The part that took the longest was the carving, and once the design had been copied and transferred to the back splats, that did not take very long either.

CONSTRUCTION

Use the 2in (50mm) grid drawn on the plans to make a full-size template of the back legs from a scrap of hardboard. When you have sawn out the template, mark on it the position of all the mortices that have to be cut in the leg (Fig. 1).

Position the template on the 2in (50mm) thick plank and jockey it about to find the most economical cutting pattern. Ignore the knots. This is a very strong chair, and unless there is a huge knot in a critical place, I would ignore them when laying out the template and aim for an economical cut.

Saw the legs to shape, using a jig saw fitted with a (T144D) blade and with maximum orbital action. This speeds up the job and the blade is less likely to stray from the vertical.

Plane up the front and sides of the back legs. The gentle curve in the back face can be smoothed with a spokeshave (see page 152) or with a block plane used across the grain, followed by coarse sandpaper used with a curved block.

Saw out the 2in (50mm) square front legs and then cut out all the rails and stretchers. Remember when you are cutting that the backrests are all through-tenoned. They will, therefore, have to be cut to slightly more than 20in (508mm) wide overall. The remaining tenons are all 1½in (38mm) long.

Shaping the back legs

The back legs taper inwards from the seat (Fig. 2). The taper is cut from the outside of the legs. From 2in (50mm) at the seat, the legs taper to 1¼in (30mm) at the top. Mark in the taper on each leg. Place them together to ensure that the legs make a

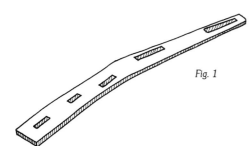

Fig. 1

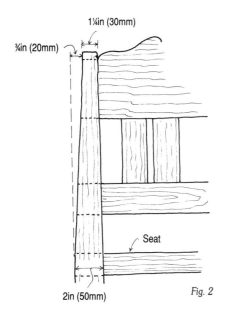

1¼in (30mm)

¾in (20mm)

Seat

2in (50mm)

Fig. 2

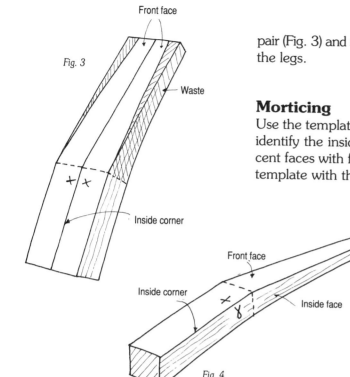

Fig. 3

Front face

Waste

Inside corner

pair (Fig. 3) and saw off the waste from each leg. Finish smoothing the legs.

Morticing

Use the template to mark out the mortices. To avoid confusion, identify the inside corner of each back leg, and mark the adjacent faces with face side and face edge marks (Fig. 4). Align the template with the bottom of the legs and pencil in the position

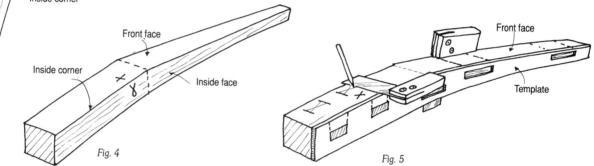

Front face

Inside corner

Inside face

Fig. 4

Front face

Template

Fig. 5

of each mortice. For mortices that face forwards, use the inside face of the leg to brace your set square (Fig. 5). For the longer tenons that reach across the back, rest the set square against the front face of the leg.

Set the points of your mortice gauge to ⅜in (9mm) and the fence to the same, and scribe in the mortices as appropriate. Both ends of a through mortice have to be scribed using the same bearing face for the gauge at each end.

All the stopped mortices can be routed out quickly and cleanly, using a router fitted with a ⅜in (9mm) cutter. I was a little anxious about using the router for the through mortices, because the outside of the joint is open to scrutiny and I did not want to see any signs of machining in the finished product. I ended up doing all the morticing by hand, and it did not take long to complete.

To cut a through mortice by hand, chop out and completely finish one side, and then turn over the leg and start on the opposite. Take a lot of care with the edges of the mortice, particularly where they will be seen, and try not to stray over the scribe lines or bruise the ends of the mortice by levering against them with the chisel. I started by cutting the joint-facing side first and excavated well past the half-way mark, so that work on the exit side was kept to a minimum.

Rails and stretchers

Cut out all the rails and stretchers, and mark and saw the tenons. The chair has a virtually square framework, so the rails and stretchers on the sides are all the same length and the distance between the shoulders for the rails and stretchers that link the front legs is the same as that between the shoulders, for the backrests, and the seat rail.

Remember when you are scribing the tenons, that the face sides of the rails and stretchers are finished flush with the front or outside face of the legs (Fig. 6). Only the rear seat rail is flush with the back face of the chair legs (Fig. 7).

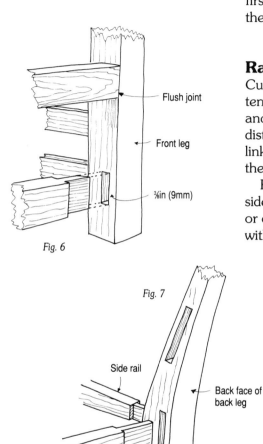

Flush joint

Front leg

⅜in (9mm)

Fig. 6

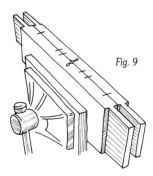

Side rail

Rear seat rail

Fig. 7

Back face of back leg

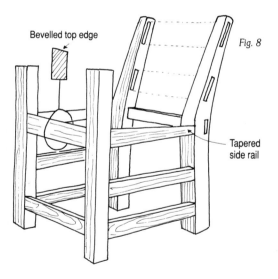

Bevelled top edge

Fig. 8

Tapered side rail

Fig. 9

When you have cut the tenons, trim the top edge of the front seat rail to the angle shown in the plans and saw down the side rails so that they extend this angle when they are fitted between the legs (Fig. 8). Plane the saw cut smooth.

Take the two wide pieces of the backrest, which hold the three carved splats, hold them together in the vice and mark the positions for the six shallow mortices that will hold the splats (Fig. 9). Cut out the mortices.

The carved back

The chair that is featured in the photographs has two different samples of carving on the back. The central splat has a simple motif, featuring a raised stalk with a few leaves and berries scattered about (Fig. 10). The splats flanking it display a slightly more complex carving of foliage (Fig. 11).

Fig. 10

Fig. 11

These splats are tenoned into the backrest, but unless you are very confident in your carving, it is probably a good idea to postpone sawing the tenons until you have finished the carving.

The two designs were carved with a narrow veiner, a V parting tool, two gouges and a penknife. In addition, I made a couple of narrow gouges that I could slip into the awkward crevices between the leaves. (I have included some simple instructions for making gouges and chisels on pages 156–7).

CARVING

For those with no experience of woodcarving, it is probably best to keep the design as simple and bold as you can. Draw your design on the first splat. If you are going to repeat the same design three times, the easiest way of transferring the design is to blacken the reverse side of the drawing with a soft pencil, and then pencil over the design when the paper is positioned accurately over the splat. Draw a border about ¼in (6mm) wide around the edge of the splat to contain the design (Fig. 12).

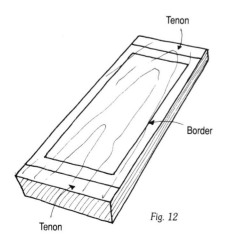

Tenon

Border

Tenon

Fig. 12

This is a relief carving. You need only sink the background by about ⅛in (4mm); all the other carving – the rounding, veining and so on – are completed within that depth.

Arrange an angle-poise lamp near your vice and position the bulb close to the bench, directing it to give a low light. This will highlight the carving and help you to see the effect of your work.

Place the splat in the vice and take the small veiner chisel. You can either hold it with both hands and carve around the design, or you can tap it around the edge of the design using a light mallet. I favour using the mallet, because it is easier to control, particularly where there are variations in grain.

As you use the veiner, tilt it slightly so that the bottom of the blade is almost undercutting the line you are carving (Fig. 13). When you come to the border, carve along that as well, and, as the veiner nears a corner, draw the handle slightly into the panel so that the tip of the blade finishes the cut with a mitre (Figs. 14 and 15).

Veiner held at slight angle

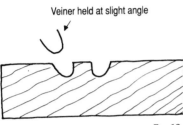

Fig. 13

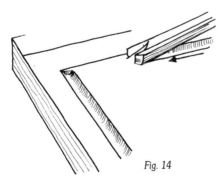

Fig. 14

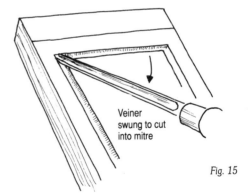

Veiner swung to cut into mitre

Fig. 15

When you have worked around the outside of the design, work around it again, this time using the V parting chisel. Do not carve any deeper. The purpose of this second cut is to sharpen up the outline, and there may be parts of your design where it is easier to chop downwards with a gouge or knife than to work around it with the chisel. Do not carve around the borders of the splat, it will look stronger with the radius left by the veiner.

Now take a ½in (12mm) no. 3 gouge and remove the waste. Use small strokes of the gouge so that each movement removes its own little chip of wood. This gouge will clear the waste from the open areas of the groundwork. When you are faced with clearing the groundwork in awkward corners, you will have to use whatever tool you can find that will do the job. This is the slow and awkward part of the work, and it is best to be thorough, so that you do not find yourself going back over your work to tighten up sloppy chiselling after the final carving is completed.

From here onwards carving is all fun. Keep your light source low, for as you will have realized by now, it is the shadows that give the carving its strength. What you take away is just as important as what is left. But make sure that you do not get side-tracked into carving too much detail. This will detract from the boldness of the carving.

Stalks should be rounded at their edges (Fig. 16), and leaves should be formed slightly dipped in cross-section (Fig. 17). If you are not sure how to start, pencil some cross-sections on the carving as illustrated (Fig. 18). This will help you visualize what you are planning to do. Try to keep all your lines in rhythm to help the movement or flow of the carving and use any tools you can to achieve the effects you seek. Fig. 19 show some ways of using a gouge to carve leaves and berries.

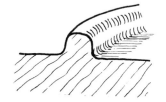

Fig. 16

Fig. 17

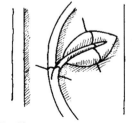

Fig. 18

Fig. 19

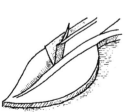

Use any suitable gouge for round forms

Cut triangles from between clusters before shaping

Carving a leaf

Undercut

Fig. 20

UNDERCUTTING

Do not undercut the design (Fig. 20). There is no scope in a carving as shallow as this for undercutting and there is, in any case, no need. The shadows surrounding a leaf, for example, will be no different if the leaf has been undercut so there is no point in trying. The danger of undercutting is that you weaken the wood and can never correct a mistake once you have carved away behind it.

Once you have carved the three panels, cut the tenons at the ends and check that they fit. Smooth the sides and back of each splat and fit the back leg assembly together to ensure that all the parts fit together.

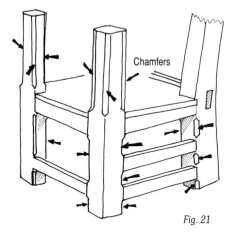

Chamfers

Fig. 21

Chamfering the legs

Both the back and front legs are chamfered (Fig. 21). The chamfering stops ½in (12mm) short each side of the mortices. The inside corner of each leg has a long chamfer running from just below the level of the seat rail to the ground. There are no chamfers on the back of the back legs or above the seat rail.

Mark the chamfers free-hand (Fig. 22). Make sure that the start and finish of each chamfer is clearly marked. Chamfering is done free-hand with a wide chisel. If you have not cut a chamfer before, take one of the front legs and place it in the vice with the inside long corner that will be chamfered sticking out of the vice and facing away from you.

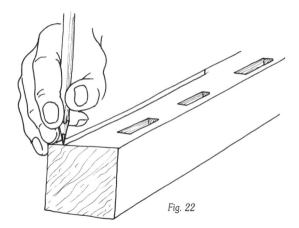

Fig. 22

Take a 1½in (38mm) chisel, make sure it is sharp and then hold it as shown in Fig. 23. Tap it with the mallet. This will give you a line to work to.

Hold the chisel at an angle as shown (Fig. 24) and slice along the edge, removing a fine regular shaving. If this is difficult turn the wood around and work from the other direction. Continue shaving until you have reached the chamfer marks. At first it may take several passes to reach the line, but as you become accustomed to using the chisel rather like a plane, you will find ways of controlling its direction and depth of cut in the way you brace the tool against the leg.

When you reach the end cut of the chamfer, lift away the chisel and carve the gentle radius to finish the cut (Fig. 25). Do not sand the chamfers – they are best left alone, however crudely they are cut.

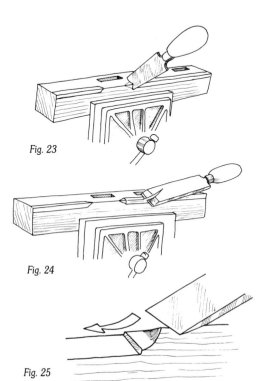

Fig. 23

Fig. 24

Fig. 25

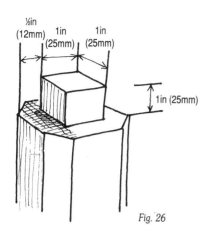

½in (12mm) 1in (25mm) 1in (25mm)

1in (25mm)

Fig. 26

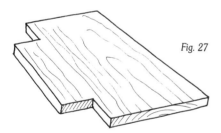

Fig. 27

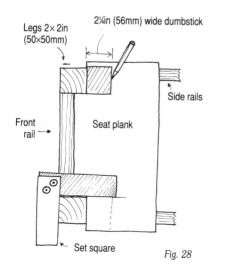

Legs 2 × 2in (50×50mm)

2¼in (56mm) wide dumbstick

Side rails

Front rail →

Seat plank

Set square

Fig. 28

Armrest tenons

At the top of each front leg there is a tenon. This is 1in (25mm) square (Fig. 26). Line up and clamp the two front legs together, and mark a shoulder-line 1in (25mm) down from the tops. Square around the legs and then, using a marking gauge, scribe the sides of the tenons. Cut them out using a tenon saw.

Gluing the chair together

This chair is glued together, and the joints are held with panel pins while the glue dries. Before gluing, check that all the joints fit. Number them and lay them on the bench ready for assembly.

Glue the front legs and stretchers together first. Run the glue around the edges of the mortices. The tenons will draw the glue into the joints as they are pressed home. When all four joints are fitted, clamp the legs together tightly, check that the structure is square and correct it if necessary. Hammer a panel pin through each mortice. You can punch the heads down later. Release the clamps.

Next, glue the back legs. This will take a little longer because of the splats, which have to be fitted (but need not be glued) before the backrest tenons can be inserted into the legs.

Then glue the four side rails and stretchers into the back legs and finish by fitting the front legs on to the ends of the stretchers.

Check for squareness and rest the chair frame on a flat surface to ensure that all four legs are level. Leave the glue to dry.

Fitting the seat

Fit the seat support that is glued and nailed to the back stretcher and is shown in the plans. The top edge of the support is planed to suit the angle of the seat, which slopes down towards the back of the chair.

The seat is made from three pieces of ½in (12mm) thick board. The front board is notched around the legs and nailed to the front and side rails (Fig. 27). There is a small ¼in (6mm) lip at the front where the seat overhangs the rail, and it overhangs the side rails by the same amount. Leave the overhang at the sides untrimmed until all the seat planks are fixed in place.

The notches for the front legs are marked out using a 2¼in (56mm) wide dumb stick (Fig. 28). When the front plank is fitted, do the same at the back, this time butting the back edge of the plank against the seat rail.

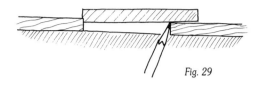

Fig. 29

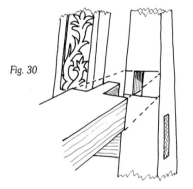

Fig. 30

⅜in (9mm) mortice chisel

Supporting wedge

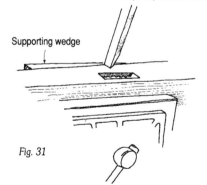

Fig. 31

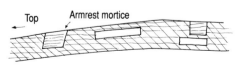

Top   Armrest mortice

Section through the back leg

Fig. 32

Fit the middle plank last. This should be a tight fit, so make sure the glue holding the tenons is set before fitting this plank. Mark it as illustrated (Fig. 29) and shave it down so it is a fraction oversize. Lift the inside edge of the two outer planks, place the centre plank between them, insert some glue into the joints and press them all down. They should click into position.

Nail the planks to the rails, supporting the rails with an iron block held beneath the rail when you are hammering. Punch the nail heads below the surface of the seat. Lastly, saw and then plane the sides of the seat planks so they are straight and smooth.

Fitting the armrests

The armrests are tenoned into the back legs (Fig. 30) and are morticed to fit over the front leg tenons.

Mark the positions for the stopped mortices in the back legs and scribe them with the mortice gauge points set to ⅜in (9mm).

Support the underside of the back legs and chop out the mortices, which are 1in (25mm) deep (Fig. 31). Take care not to round the top edges of the mortices, which will be seen when the armrests are fitted, and, if you can, angle the ends of the mortices as illustrated in Fig. 32 to accommodate the slope of the back legs. Now mark the tenons on the ends of the armrests, using the same gauge point setting that you used on the legs.

Clamp the first armrest in position, holding it to the front leg and the back leg, and pencil on its side the shoulder angle for the tenon (Fig. 33).

Set the angle bevel to this angle and mark around the shoulders (Fig. 34).

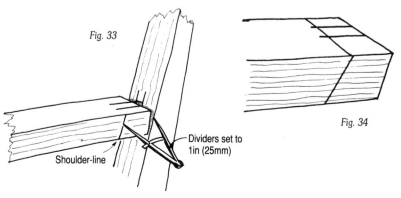

Fig. 33

Shoulder-line

Dividers set to 1in (25mm)

Fig. 34

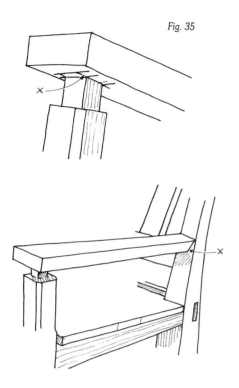

Fig. 35

Fig. 36

Cut the tenons and fit them. Once you have pressed them in position, you will find it is impossible to push them right home because the front leg tenons are lifting the front ends too high, so the joint will be open at the bottom.

Press in the tenon at the back until the top shoulder is touching the back leg, then use a pencil to mark the location of the front leg tenon. As a guide, the inside edge of the front leg should be flush with the inside edge of the armrest, and in side view, the mortice will be a little closer to the front than it is when you measure it (Fig. 35). The distance is more or less equivalent to the size of the open crack at the back legs (Fig. 36).

Mark out the mortice and chop it out. With a mortice as wide as this, it will be a help if you can cut out the majority of the waste with a flat bit fitted into an electric drill. Do not drill too far and clean out the corners with a bevel-edged chisel.

Fit the armrest and trim the joints until they all close up. If you have to make adjustments, make them to the mortice over the front legs, because adjustment work here or packing pieces slipped into the joint will neither show nor significantly weaken the joint.

Cut the armrests to shape with a jig saw and smooth the sawn edge with a spokeshave and chisel, before gluing the armrests into place. When the glue has dried, finish the smoothing and rounding of the armrests and all the other hard edges you find, except the chamfers.

Punch all the nail heads below the surface of the wood and fill the holes with two-part filler. Sand the chair, using an orbital sander fitted with 220 grit paper.

FINISHING

Stain the chair using Colron spirit stains. A combination of Canadian Cedar with a dash of American Walnut and diluted with English Light Oak will give the chair a warm, rich colour. Apply the stain with a brush, controlling the spread of the stain with a rag held in your other hand. When the stain has dried, brush on two or three coats of button polish shellac. Leave this to dry and then rub down all the surfaces with 000 wire wool.

Finish with black or brown quick-drying wax.

BUREAU

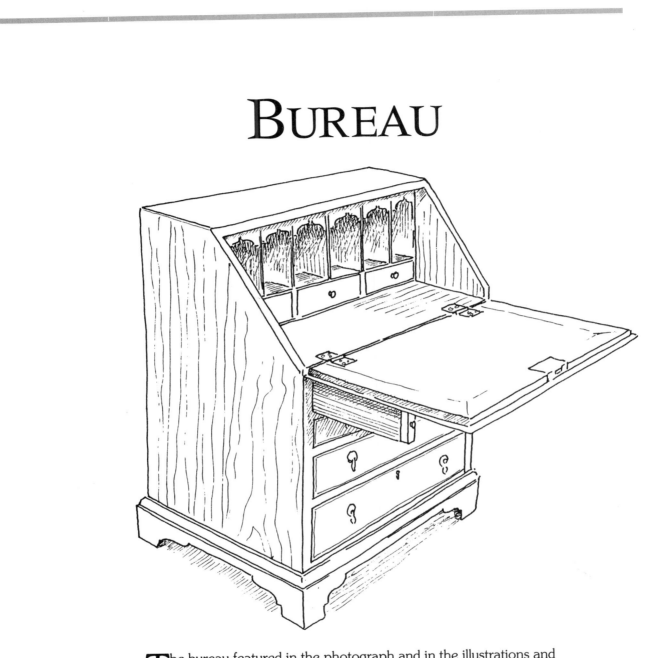

The bureau featured in the photograph and in the illustrations and instructions in this section is a very small, cottage bureau, only 26in (660mm) wide and 22in (about 560mm) deep. It is a copy of a mid-eighteenth-century bureau. There are four large drawers. The top drawer is sandwiched between the two bearers that draw out and support the fall when the bureau is open.

The inside of the desk is fitted with a nest of small drawers and pigeon-holes. Quite often the maker will have concealed some secret drawers and compartments inside the nest, and this is no exception – there are at least three in this bureau.

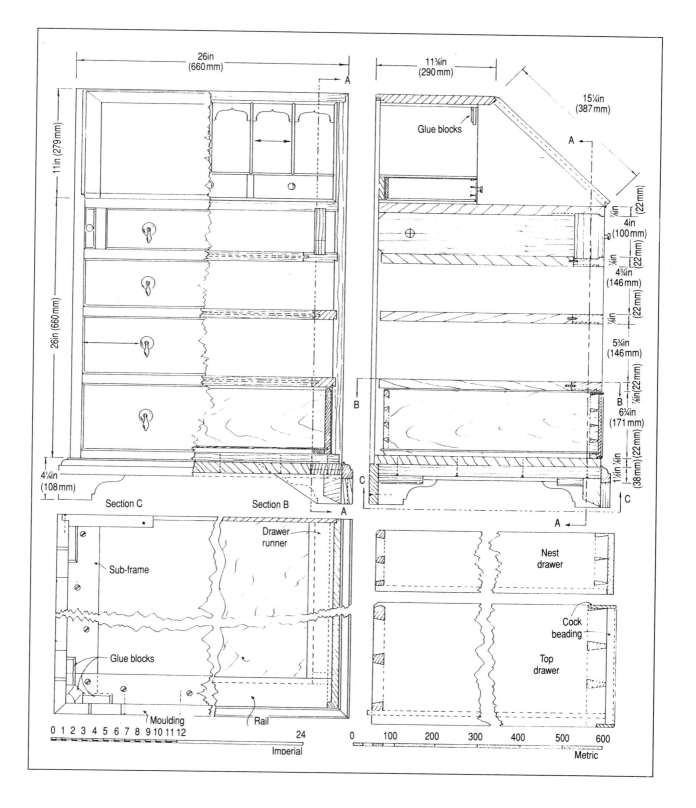

Glue blocks

26in
(660mm)

11⅜in
(290mm)

15¼in
(387mm)

11in (279mm)

26in (660mm)

4¼in
(108mm)

⅞in (22mm)
4in (100mm)
⅞in (22mm)
4¾in (146mm)
⅞in (22mm)
5¾in (146mm)
⅞in (22mm)
6¾in (171mm)
⅞in (22mm)
1½in (38mm)

Section C
Section B

Sub-frame

Drawer
runner

Glue blocks

Moulding
Rail

Nest
drawer

Cock
beading

Top
drawer

0 1 2 3 4 5 6 7 8 9 10 11 12   24
Imperial

0   100   200   300   400   500   600
Metric

Cherry wood has been used for making the carcass, drawer fronts and fall of this bureau, as well as the fronts to the pigeon-holes, drawers, the shelf and fall. Pine has been used for the bottom, plywood for the back and for the drawer bottoms, and oak for the sides and backs of the drawers and for the hidden work inside the pigeon-holes.

Fig. 1 shows some of the construction details. The main carcass is dovetailed together, the bottom to the sides with lap dovetails, and double lapped dovetails at the top. The drawer runners are slotted or housed into the sides, and a dovetailed slot holds the ends of the drawer rails and prevents the sides from bowing out. A plywood dust board is retained by grooves worked in the runners and rails.

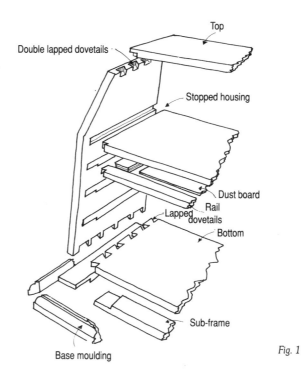

Top

Double lapped dovetails

Stopped housing

Dust board

Rail

Lapped dovetails

Bottom

Sub-frame

Base moulding

Fig. 1

Underneath and glued to the main carcass is a lightly made pine framework on to which is glued the base moulding. This, in turn, supports the bracket feet, which are glued and nailed to the moulding, and mitred at the front corners. Wooden glue blocks support the brackets at the front, while the back legs are lapped to hold a pine bracket, which is glued to the bottom boards.

The fall is made from three planks, clamped at the ends to hold them flat. A simple thumbnail moulding is worked around the top edge and sides, which overlaps on to the sides and top of the desk.

The drawers are dovetailed together, and those in the nest have their bottoms nailed into rebates at the front and sides.

Included in the sketches of the joints are some alternative methods, which are quicker and easier than those just described. I have not included instructions as the drawings are more or less self-explanatory, and the work consists mainly of routing, rebating, gluing and nailing. The end result should be perfectly satisfactory and not unlike many country bureaux that I have worked on in my workshop.

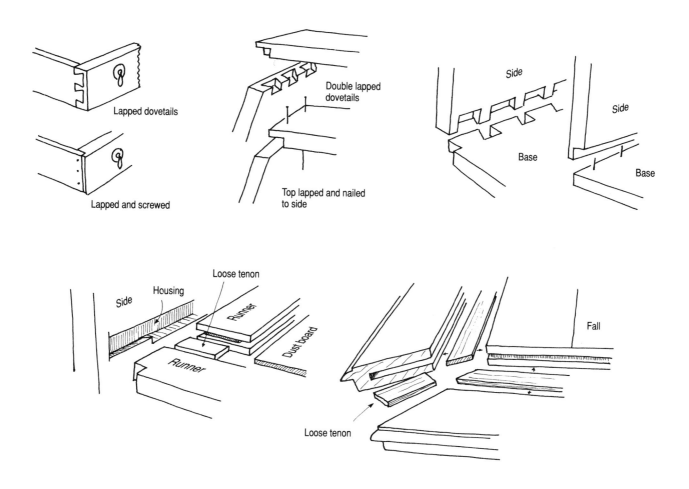

CONSTRUCTION

The main carcass is put together first (Fig. 2). This is composed of the sides, the base, the drawer rails, the top shelf and the top, which are all made from planks ⅞in (22mm) thick. While you are at this stage and before you cut out any other wood for the sides or drawer fronts, select enough clean, quarter-sawn timber for the fall. Cut it out, plane it smooth, but not to thickness, and stack it in a warm place, with thin battens between each layer, to let it dry out.

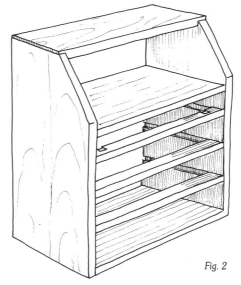

Fig. 2

Make up the sides first. I was able to make them 22½in (572mm) wide using three planks, and left ½in (12mm) extra for shrinkage at the back edge, which could be trimmed just before assembly.

The sides are shot and joined using a loose tongue, in the same way that the top of the side table was put together (see pages 59–60). Cut the planks roughly to size and saw the slope at the front edge of each side as well, so that when you groove the edges of the planks with the biscuit jointer you can see where the slope is and can stop the jointer well before it reaches the edge. It would be a pity to show the loose tongue in the grain at the sides of the fall.

Glue and clamp the sides. When the glue has hardened, plane the inside face smooth, or at least that part that is on show inside the desk and plane the outside face flat.

By referring to the plans, mark in and cut the bottom line of the side, using the front edge as your straightedge. Saw the bottom line with a hand saw. This is a long cut, but as long as you position yourself comfortably over the line and use the saw gently, it should not wander off the line. It is quicker to saw by hand slowly and accurately, than to use a power saw, such as a jig saw or skill saw, and then plane up afterwards. Trim the opposite side in the same way.

Make up the top plank from a couple of clean grained planks of cherry. The bottom plank can be made from pine, with just a 2½in (65mm) strip of cherry glued to its front edge (Fig. 3).

Plane them smooth and square the ends with a sharp hand plane. Mark on the back inside edge of each board the rebate for the ¼in (6mm) plywood backboard, and cut it out using the router.

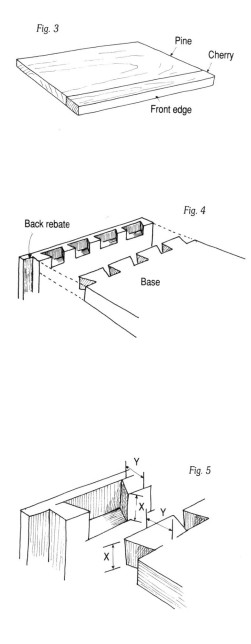

Fig. 3

Pine

Cherry

Front edge

Fig. 4

Back rebate

Base

Fig. 5

Dovetailing the carcass

The first joints to cut are the bottom joints that hold the sides and base together (Fig. 4). Once they are glued together, these dovetails are virtually invisible. A critic might obtain some idea of how well they are cut by removing the bottom drawer and peering at the line of the joint, but not much will be visible, and everywhere else the joint is concealed. Underneath, they are hidden by the sub-frame on to which the base moulding and bracket feet are mounted, and at the side the ends of the dove-tails are concealed by the lap. So you do not need to worry when you cut these joints. Dovetails have enormous mechanical strength, and even badly cut dovetails, with yawning gaps filled with glue and sawdust, will be amply strong enough. Use the dovetail cutting here for practice. There are plenty of demonstration dovetails to cut later.

CUTTING LAP DOVETAILS

Figs. 4 and 5 show a row of lapped dovetails. You will notice that only two marking gauge settings are used. One setting, X, is the thickness of the bottom plank. The setting Y is equal to the length of the dovetail (from the shoulder-line to the end of the tail), which, you will see, will also give you the lap-line scribed on the bottom edge of the side plank.

You will need a cutting gauge and a marking gauge, and there are instructions for making your own gauges, included in the tool section of the book (see pages 155–6). Set the cutting gauge to Y, and the marking gauge, which has the point to the setting X. Use the gauges to scribe the lines. The gauge set to Y can be used on both sides of the ends of the bottom plank, as well as being used for scribing the lap. X setting is used only once, as a shoulder-line on the inside of the side.

Take a set square and square around the ends of the bottom plank.

Fig. 6

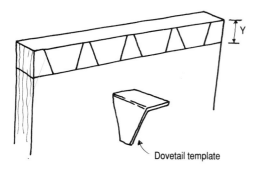

Dovetail template

MARKING THE DOVETAILS

These are the first to be marked. Fig. 6 shows how they should look. I mark mine free-hand, but it is very easy to cut a tin or cardboard template and use this to give you a consistent angle. Space the dovetails regularly. The dovetails can be quite wide but not more than 3in (75mm), and the pins (the parts that are inserted between the tails) need be no more than ½in (12mm) at their widest point. Notice that these are not through dovetails. The dovetails extend only three-quarters of the width of the side planks and are concealed from the side by the ¼in (6mm) lap. The distance from the shoulder-line to the end of the tails is about three-quarters of the width of the side plank.

When you have drawn the tails on the face of the bottom plank, use a set square to continue the lines of the tails across the edge of the plank (Fig. 7). This will help you to saw the dovetail sides accurately.

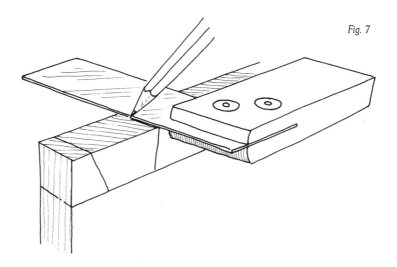

Fig. 7

SAWING THE DOVETAILS

The best way to saw a row of dovetails is to clamp a straight plank to the back of the board, positioning it just below the shoulder-line of the dovetails, and then to clamp the two together in the vice. The bottom board is so wide that you will need this support when you are sawing the dovetails (Fig. 8). When you are tightening the vice, tilt the end of the bottom board until one side of each dovetail is vertical. If you do this, you can use the saw vertically, and this will make the sawing easier and give better results.

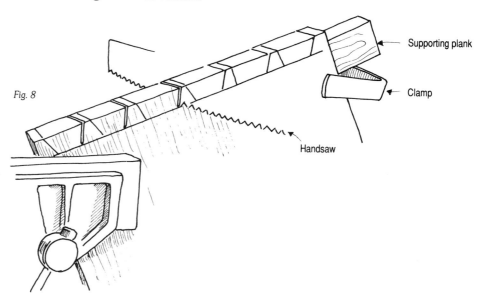

Fig. 8

Supporting plank

Clamp

Handsaw

When you have sawn one side of the dovetails, re-adjust the angle at which they are clamped in the vice and saw the other sides, stopping the saw cut as you reach the shoulder-lines. Remove the supporting plank, and saw off the waste wedge at each end of the plank (Fig. 9).

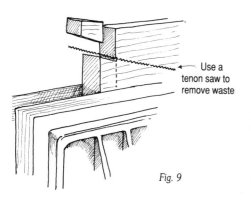

Use a tenon saw to remove waste

Fig. 9

FINISHING THE DOVETAILS

The waste between the tails is not so readily removed. First, take a coping saw and saw away as much of the waste as you can. Leave between a $\frac{1}{16}$in (1.5mm) and $\frac{1}{8}$in (4mm) waste between the saw cut and the shoulder-line. This allows some latitude for sloppy cutting and leaves enough to chisel away easily (Fig. 10).

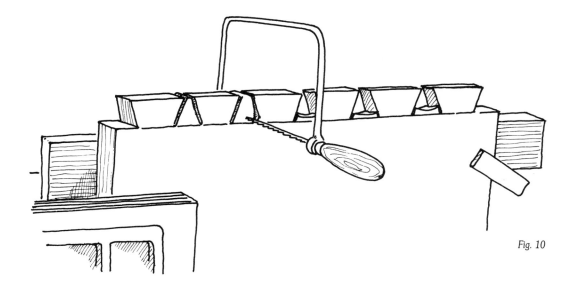

Fig. 10

Lay the board on a flat plank and take a ½in (12mm) or slightly narrower bevel-edged chisel and a light mallet. Place the chisel in the shoulder-line, hold it vertical and hit it with the mallet. Two blows should be enough to remove the waste and reach a little past the middle of the plank. If the chisel bruises or scores the wood past the shoulder-line, you must either sharpen the chisel or take finer cuts.

Repeat this right along the row of tails. Then turn the board over and finish the opposite side in the same way. If you tilt the chisel slightly to undercut the shoulder-line (as shown in Fig. 11), you will not have to level the shoulder between the dovetails afterwards.

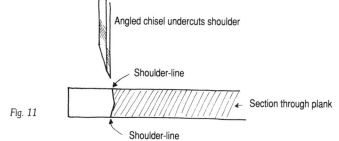

Fig. 11

When you have cut out the tails, you can scribe around them to mark the pins. The dovetailing so far may have taken you an hour, but you can expect that with a little practice you should be able to complete cutting a 2ft (610mm) row of dovetails in about 15 minutes, so things will speed up.

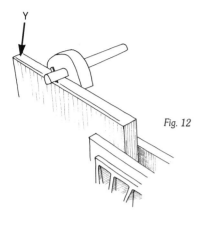

Fig. 12

MARKING THE PINS

Place one side of the bureau in the vice, bottom edge upwards and with the inside face facing the bench. Using the inside face as the edge to work from, scribe the Y gauge along the bottom edge (Fig. 12). This will give you the lap-line for the dovetails. Now use the second gauge, X, to scribe the depth line, resting the fence against the bottom edge (Fig. 13).

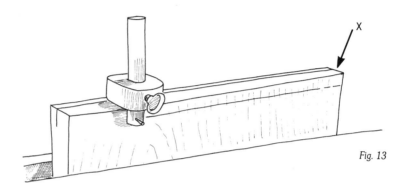

Fig. 13

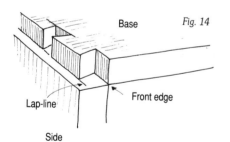

Base   Fig. 14

Lap-line

Front edge

Side

Place the bottom plank in position, with its dovetails resting on the edge of the side plank. You may need to prop the opposite end of the bottom plank with some blocks to keep it level. Line the ends of the dovetails with the scribed lap-line. A quick inspection should show that the shoulder-line of the dovetails is directly above the inside edge of the side (Fig. 14). Of course, some of the shoulders will be badly chopped out and will obviously be wrong, but if there is an overall error, which might have been caused by the gauge being moved, you should check the accuracy of the lap-line, and when you are sure you have made a mistake, change it.

You can now mark the pins, by poking a knife between the dovetails and scribing the bottom of the side plank. But if you want to make a really tight joint, jog the dovetails a little past the lap-line, perhaps by no more than 1/16in (1.5mm), and then mark their position with a sharp knife or fine saw blade (Fig. 15).

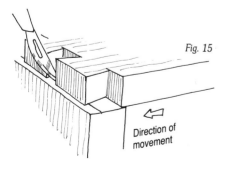

Fig. 15

Direction of movement

CUTTING THE PINS

Turn the side around in the vice so that the inside face shows, and use a set square and pencil to draw in the sides of the pins (Fig. 16).

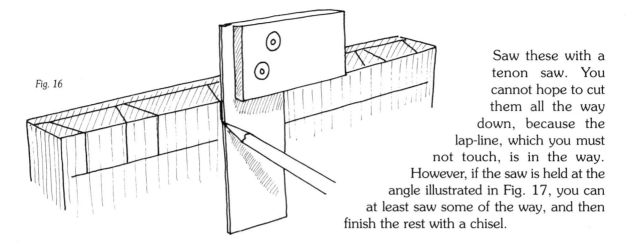

Fig. 16

Saw these with a tenon saw. You cannot hope to cut them all the way down, because the lap-line, which you must not touch, is in the way. However, if the saw is held at the angle illustrated in Fig. 17, you can at least saw some of the way, and then finish the rest with a chisel.

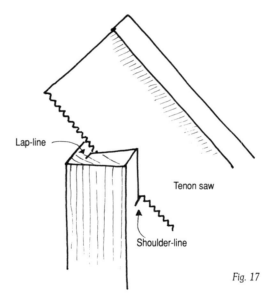

Lap-line

Tenon saw

Shoulder-line

Fig. 17

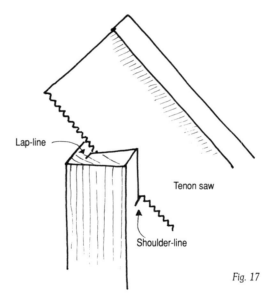

Fig. 18

Place the side on the bench, with the outer face protected by a sheet of smooth hardboard. Clamp it with a G-clamp at each edge, close to the shoulder-line of the pins. Take a ⅝in (15mm) firmer or morticing chisel and a mallet, and chop back the waste, stopping when you approach the lap-line (Fig. 18). Because you are chopping end-grain, the waste will fall away, and you will easily be able to tell when you have gone far enough. Avoid chopping right down to the lap-line. Stop about ⅛in (4mm) away and finish off by hand when the side plank is vertical again. If you carry on chopping right to the lap-line, pieces will fall away on the wrong side of the line and the joint will be spoilt. This does not really matter on these joints,

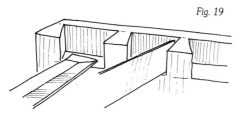

Fig. 19

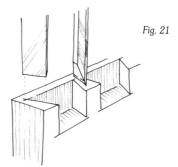

Fig. 20

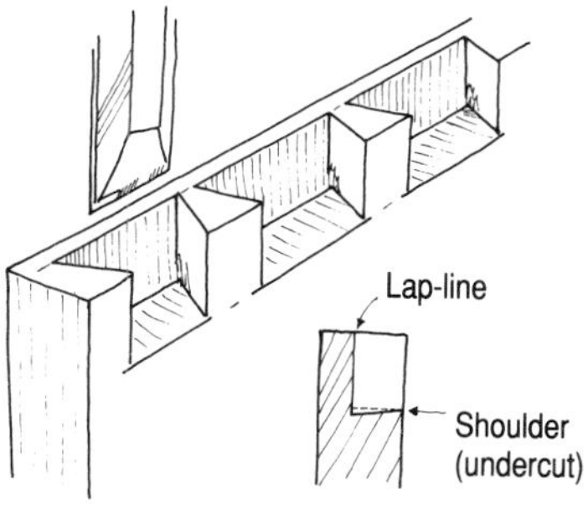

Lap-line

Shoulder
(undercut)

because the sub-frame holding the bracket feet will conceal your work, but you might as well practise cutting good joints here, because your work will certainly be seen (and probably inspected) on the ends of the drawers.

You will be unable to complete the trimming with a mallet and chisel. When all the waste areas on this row have been chopped out, return the side to the vice, face side farthest from you, and use a bevel-edged chisel to clean up the work (Fig. 19).

It will be easy to trim down to the lap-line and the shoulder-line. Undercut the shoulder-line slightly, but try to keep the lap-line vertical (Fig. 20). When the main area of waste is cleared, use the chisel as illustrated in Fig. 21 to trim away the sides of the pins until you reach the shoulder. Snip off the shavings at the shoulder with a knife and repeat all along the row of pins.

Fig. 21

FITTING THE DOVETAILS

Before trying out the joint, take the bottom plank, clamp it to the bench and chisel a slight bevel to the inside edge of each tail. This will help the joint slide together (Fig. 22).

Place the dovetails over the pins and tap them into place with a hammer, protecting the bottom board with a straight batten. If the pins are too large and the joint refuses to mesh, trim the pins that are too large or that are the wrong shape. Cut the dovetail joint at the other end of the bottom plank

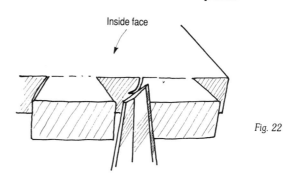

Inside face

Fig. 22

Double lapped dovetails at the top of the bureau

Mark and plane up the front edge of the top plank (Fig. 23). You will notice that the edge has two angles. Its lower angle should be at right angles or slightly less than right angles to the angle of the fall. This is easily found by marking out the position of the

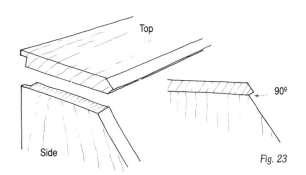

Fig. 23

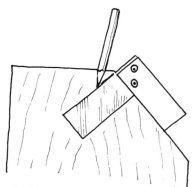

Fig. 24

top on the side plank and then, using the set square, pencilling in its lower edge (Fig. 24). Adjust this angle a little, so that it is a little less than right angles, and this will enable the fall completely to seal the desk when it is closed. Transfer the angle to a sliding bevel, and use this to help you plane the angle on the top plank.

Fig. 25 shows an example of this joint. Once it is assembled, both the tails and the pins are hidden.

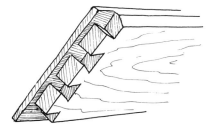

MARKING AND CUTTING THE PINS

The pins are cut in the side planks. Mark the position of the top plank on the side planks. Scribe in the shoulder-line from the top edge of the side plank downwards, which is equivalent to the thickness of the top plank, less ¼in (6mm) to allow for the ¼in (6mm) lap (Fig. 26).

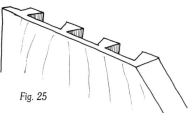

Fig. 25

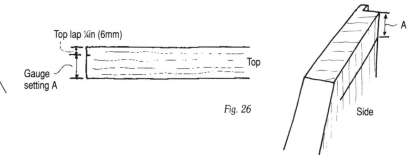

Fig. 26

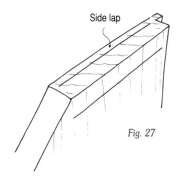

Side lap

Fig. 27

Scribe a second line on the top edge of the side plank, which could be the same setting as before (but check), and this will give you the length of dovetail and the lap at the edge of the side (Fig. 27).

You do not want the joint to finish too close to the front edge of the top, so, bearing this in mind, mark in the dovetail shapes on the top edge of the side plank (Fig. 28). Make the pins wide. When you are cutting out the dovetails later on, it is easier to have widths of at least ⅜in (9mm) at the narrow points of the pins. Use a set square to mark down the sides of the pins (Fig. 29).

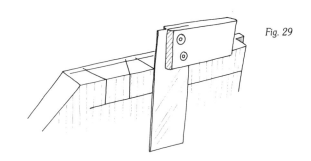

Fig. 29

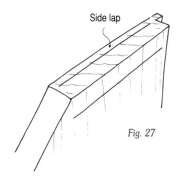

Fig. 28

The pins are finished first. Use a tenon saw to cut the waste from beside the pins, and then chisel away the waste in exactly the same way as when the recesses for the ordinary lapped dovetails were chopped out (see pages 86–7). Remember that this time it is the pins that you are cutting out (Fig. 30).

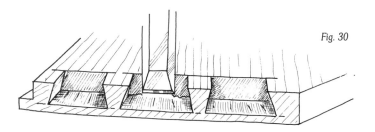

Fig. 30

Finish the pins perfectly. They should be neat and crisp. The bottom of the recess should be at the scribe line and slightly undercut.

Repeat on the opposite side, using the same gauge settings.

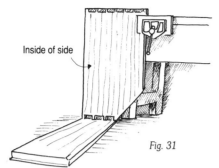

Inside of side

Fig. 31

FITTING THE DOVETAILS

When both sides are ready, take one, and place it upside down in the vice, in position on top of the underside of the top plank. The top plank can rest on the floor, and, with a little adjustment, you can place the two in perfect alignment (Fig. 31).

Take a sharp pencil and mark in the angle of the pins inside each cavity, where they touch the top plank (Fig. 32).

Lift the side plank away, and complete the marking of the dovetails free-hand. Use the cutting gauge to scribe in the lap-line on the edge and also scribe in the shoulder-line for the dovetails (Fig. 33).

Saw and chisel out the spaces for the pins between the dovetails (you are actually cutting the dovetails now) in the same way as you cut the pins (Fig. 34).

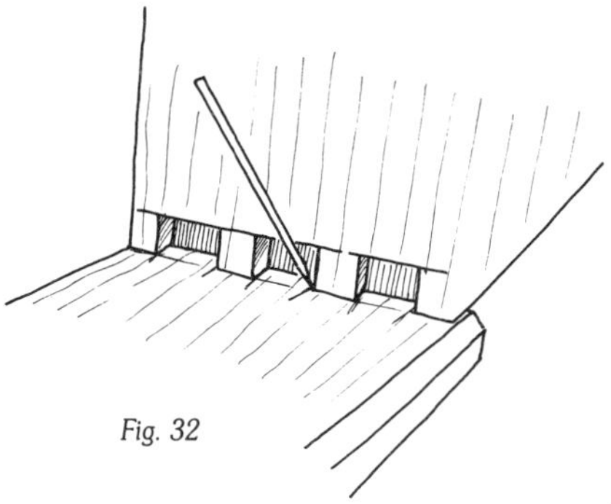

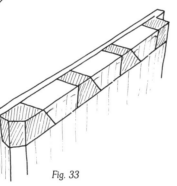

Fig. 32

Fig. 33

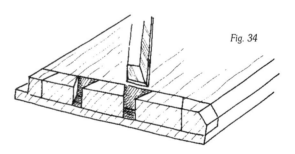

Fig. 34

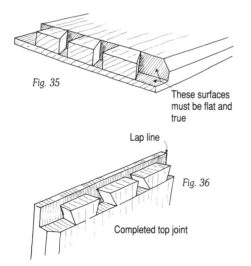

Fig. 35

These surfaces must be flat and true

Lap line

Fig. 36

Completed top joint

Cut away the waste at each end of the row of tails. Take care when you are doing this that you keep to the line. If you undercut the shoulder at the front edge of the top plank, it will leave a gap that will be seen when the fall is opened (Fig. 35).

Finally, set the router to the lap-line on the edge of the top board and rout the rebate to the lap-line (Fig. 36). You may need to trim the lap with a rebate plane to achieve a perfect joint.

Fit the joint. You may need to make some adjustments before the joint slips together perfectly, but you should not be too anxious because unless you have made a gross error, any looseness will be taken up by the glue, and when the glue has set, no one will ever know.

Repeat at the other end.

The main carcass joints have now been completed. The joints for the ends of the drawer rails, the shelf and the housings for the drawer runners remain to be done. In addition, before the carcass can be fitted together, the shallow housings that hold the divisions between the lopers and the top drawer must be routed out.

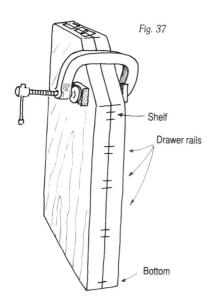

Fig. 37

Shelf

Drawer rails

Bottom

Fitting the shelf, drawer rails, drawer runners and dust boards

Join together some smooth, clean wood for the shelf, and choose some straight-grained wood for the rails. Cut these to size and plane them smooth.

Take the two sides, line them up and clamp them together, and mark on the front edges the positions for the shelf and the drawer rails (Fig. 37).

Separate the two sides and, with a set square, straightedge and ruler, extend the lines across the sides. Use a ruler to check that the lines of the drawer runners are parallel with the bottom of the sides. It is unwise to rely solely on the set square for accuracy. Use a marking gauge to scribe in the end point of the slot, which is stopped ½in (12mm) before it reaches the edges of the side (Fig. 38).

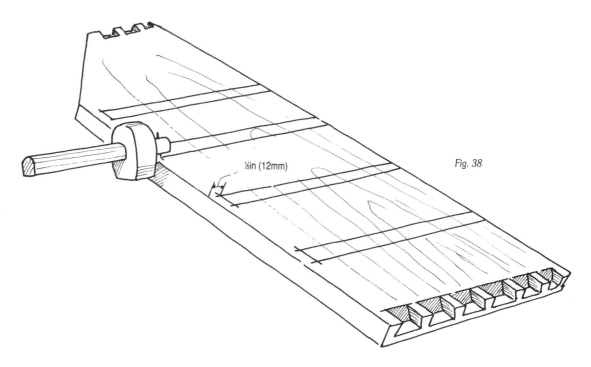

½in (12mm)

Fig. 38

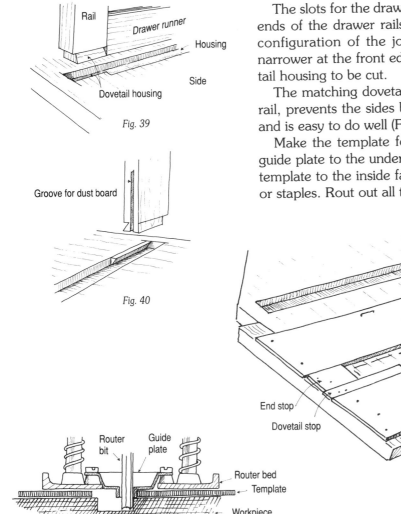

Fig. 39

Groove for dust board

Fig. 40

Fig. 42

Router bit
Guide plate
Router bed
Template
Workpiece

Fig. 43

The slots for the drawer runners and most of the slots for the ends of the drawer rails are cut by router. Fig. 39 shows the configuration of the joint, and you will see that the slot is narrower at the front edge of the bureau to allow for the dovetail housing to be cut.

The matching dovetail, which is cut on the underside of the rail, prevents the sides bowing outwards. This is a simple joint and is easy to do well (Fig. 40).

Make the template for routing these slots (Fig. 41). Fit the guide plate to the underside of the router (Fig. 42) and nail the template to the inside face of the bureau with some panel pins or staples. Rout out all the slots in both sides of the bureau.

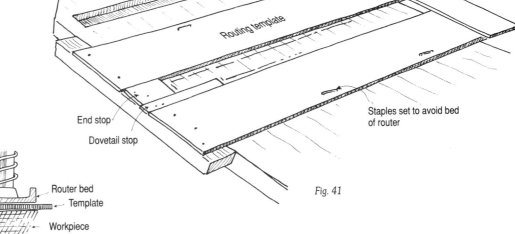

Routing template

End stop

Dovetail stop

Staples set to avoid bed of router

Fig. 41

When the slots are cut, take a chisel and chop out the dovetail housing at the end of the slots where the drawer rails fit (Fig. 43).

Cut and fit the rails, taking the shoulder-lines from the shelf or bottom board (Fig. 44). When the rails are fitted, mark the position for the dividers that sit between the top rail and the shelf. These are fitted into shallow – ¼in (6mm) – housings in the top of the drawer rail and matching housings that are cut into the underside of the shelf. Make the top housings much longer than necessary. They need to extend back for at least the width of the dividers, about 4in (100mm), so that the dividers can be slipped

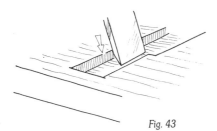

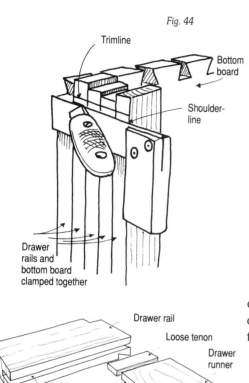

Fig. 44

Trimline

Bottom board

Shoulder-line

Drawer rails and bottom board clamped together

into position after the carcass, drawer rails, shelf and top are glued together (Fig. 45). It is really difficult to fit these dividers if you forget to cut long housings.

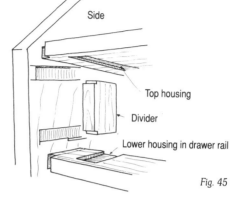

Side

Top housing

Divider

Lower housing in drawer rail

Fig. 45

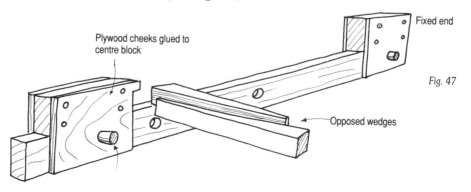

Drawer rail

Loose tenon

Drawer runner

³⁄₁₆in (5mm)

Fig. 46

Run a ³⁄₁₆in (5mm) groove along the inside edge of each drawer rail. This is to hold the dust boards, which separate the drawers, and it also helps locate the drawer runners, which are tenoned into the groove at the front rail (Fig. 46).

Before you assemble the main carcass, cut a piece of ³⁄₁₆in (5mm) plywood to fit into the back. Cut it square and make it a good, tidy fit. This will help to keep the carcass square while the glue is setting.

Assembling the carcass

Plan this operation carefully and complete the stages in the order described below. If you do not have enough furniture clamps to guarantee a satisfactory outcome, make some simple clamps to the designs suggested here, which are tightened by double wedges (Fig. 47).

Fixed end

Plywood cheeks glued to centre block

Fig. 47

Opposed wedges

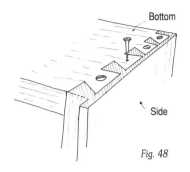

Bottom

Side

Fig. 48

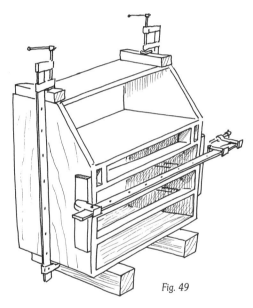

Fig. 49

Glue the bottom to one side, and hold it with a few screws driven through the dovetails into the side (Fig. 48).

Glue the other side to the bottom, screw it and support the sides with a couple of thin diagonals tacked into the rebate at the back.

Glue and fit the shelf. Clamp across the front edge and the back edge.

Fit the drawer rails. Use plenty of glue to fill any gaps in the dovetail housing not occupied by the rail. Fit the two dividers between the rail and the shelf.

Prop the carcass up on some blocks to lift it clear of the ground and to make space for the ends of the furniture clamps, which will hold the top down.

Glue and fit the top. Hold the top down with clamps, protecting the surface of the top with some wide wooden offcuts, which transfer the pressure along the whole line of lapped dovetails (Fig. 49).

Fit the back into place. Check the diagonals of the carcass and adjust it if there is some distortion, then tack the back into the rebate.

Wipe away all surplus glue with a brush and a damp rag.

Fitting the feet

Fig. 50 shows the construction details of the sub-frame, base moulding and bracket feet. The sub-frame, which is made of pine, is glued and screwed to the bottom of the bureau and left flush with the sides and front. It finishes about 1in (25mm) from

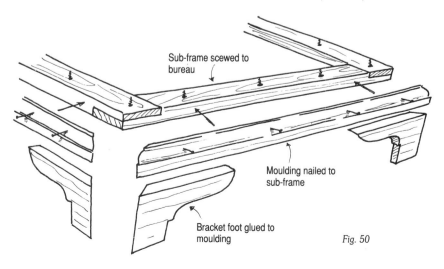

Sub-frame scewed to bureau

Moulding nailed to sub-frame

Bracket foot glued to moulding

Fig. 50

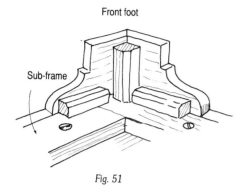

Front foot

Sub-frame

Fig. 51

the edge of the back. The base moulding is glued and nailed to the edge of the sub-frame and mitred at the front corners. The bracket feet are cut out and mitred, and then glued and screwed to the underside of the moulding. They are supported on the inside with glue blocks (Fig. 51).

Sub-frame

Make the sub-frame from any handy offcuts. The front corners are joined with a cross-halving joint, which is best sawn by hand.

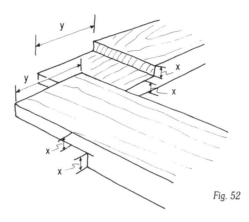

Fig. 52

If you have not cut a cross-halving joint before, mark it carefully. Fig. 52 shows how the two parts sit together, and although it is a straightforward joint, every shoulder has to be accurately marked and sawn, and the halving cuts themselves must be done with great care, otherwise the joint will not meet. If you are nervous of achieving a good match, leave some waste when you saw the two halving cuts and trim them with a chisel or beneath the router mounted in the router stand.

Glue and screw the front piece first, checking that its ends and side are flush with the carcass. Then slide the side pieces into place and screw them down (Fig. 53). The side pieces are left a little short, so that the foot support at the back can be nailed and glued to its end-grain.

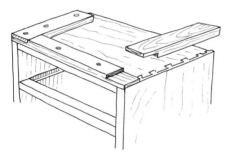

Fig. 53

Base moulding

Choose some straight-grained wood for the base moulding. Plane it on all four sides and try to keep its section regular throughout.

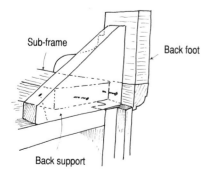

Sub-frame

Back foot

Back support

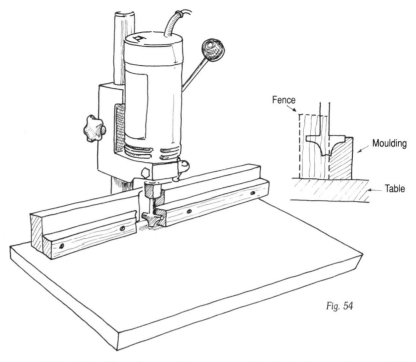

Fence

Moulding

Table

Fig. 54

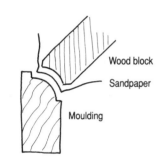

Wood block

Sandpaper

Moulding

Fig. 55

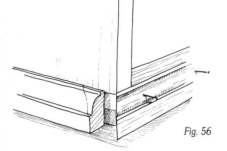

Fig. 56

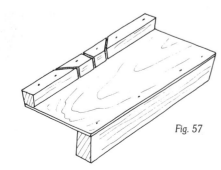

Fig. 57

Fit a ⅜in (9mm) rounding-over cutter into the router and fit the router into the router stand. Arrange a fence (Fig. 54) and cut the edge moulding in two or three passes.

Sand the moulding, supporting the sandpaper with a wooden block shaped to fit the radius. Try to keep the hard edges of the moulding sharp. If you make the wooden block slightly narrower than the overall width of the curve you are trying to sand, you are less likely to round them over (Fig. 55).

Fit the front length of the moulding first. This has a 45 degree mitre at each end. Complete sawing and trimming before marking the opposite end. When both ends of the moulding are ready, drill and then tack the moulding in place. Cut the mitre for the first return moulding on the side, and when it is trimmed to a perfect fit, cut it to length flush with the back edge of the bureau. Cut and fit the opposite return (Fig. 56).

However large the mitre you are working on, it is important that the saw you use is sharp and the plane is as keen as you can hone it. A low-angle shoulder plane is ideal for trimming mitres.

The saw guide (Fig. 57) is easy and quick to make and will be a help when making the initial cuts in narrow mouldings. You might also find the shooting board useful (Fig. 58), but I prefer to plane the joints free-hand.

Opposite: **Sewing Box, page 8**

Left: Oak Joint Stool, page 26

Below: Side Table, page 52

Below: Scandinavian Armchair, page 64

Right: Bureau, page 76

Opposite: **Bookcase, page 142**

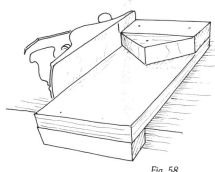

Fig. 58

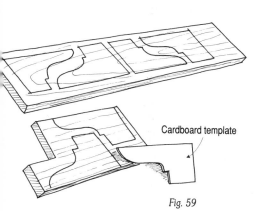

Cardboard template

Fig. 59

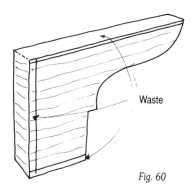

Waste

Fig. 60

When you are using the plane, press it hard against the surface of the mitre and move it really slowly. This will give you complete control. You can watch the shaving being made, you will see where the blade is cutting, and you can feel if the sole of the plane is rocking. If, after removing a few shavings, the plane still rocks, it is probable that you are applying insufficient pressure at the front of the plane and pushing the back of the plane downwards too much at the start of the stroke.

GLUING THE MOULDING

Pre-drill all the lengths ready for nailing with 1¼in (30mm) panel pins at 9in (about 229mm) centres. The front length will already be tacked in place, hold the returns in position and tap their nails so that they make dents in the edges of the sub-frame. If the nails are left in the mouldings and are slightly proud of the glued surface when you assemble, the dents in the sub-frame should help in locating the pieces.

Glue and nail the front length, and then finish by fitting the side returns. Hold the mitres with masking tape and wipe away glue from the sides of the bureau with a brush and damp rag. Punch the nails below the surface when the glue has dried.

Making the feet

The feet are made from the same wood as the carcass and the drawers, and you will not need much wood in order to cut out the six bracket feet (Fig. 59). You may be able to squeeze one or two feet on to offcuts; alternatively, with careful positioning, you can fit them on a fairly short, narrow plank.

Copy the template pattern that is drawn on the plans on to a sheet of cardboard marked with the full-scale grid. If you have not done this before, all you need to do is to mark with a cross on the full-scale grid where the line on the plans crosses the small-scale grid. Join the crosses with a straightedge where appropriate, and draw the curves free-hand. Cut out the template and use it to mark out the brackets.

Cut out the feet using a jig saw. Cut the curves as accurately as you can using a reduced orbital action setting and leave a little waste at the top, bottom and mitre edge of the feet (Fig. 60). Plane the tops square, smooth the outside (showing) faces and trim the bottom edges.

Group the feet into pairs and keep them as pairs from now on. The two least attractive feet can be put at the back of the sides and do not need to be mitred. Place the most beautiful at the front of the bureau.

Mark the mitres clearly on the top edge, front and back.

SAWING THE MITRES

These look awkward to saw, mainly because there is so little to hold in the vice. The best way I have found of coping with this is to put a piece of plank vertically in the vice and to clamp the bracket foot to the plank, with its mitre overhanging its edge (Fig. 61). Sawing the mitre is then easy, provided you know which side of the saw to watch while you are cutting it. The trick is to saw slowly: do not push or force the blade downwards, and try to develop a steady, accurate rhythm. While you are sawing, concentrate on watching the line. The saw should not cross or encroach on the line. What happens on the waste side does not matter, so do not look at it. The viewpoint can be quite awkward, but at least you are watching the right place.

Saw all the mitres before planing them square.

PLANING THE MITRES

Before you do any planing, inspect the mitres. It is possible that you have made some perfectly satisfactory cuts that require no further adjustment. Place those that need adjustment in the vice (Fig. 62) and trim them flat. Use the shoulder plane, and because you know that the blade cuts a slight hollow, cutting deeper in the middle than the sides, use this to your advantage, and place the plane so that the areas needing the most adjustment are under the centre of the blade.

When the mitres are trimmed, lay out the feet in pairs, outside face upwards, edges touching. The edges should be straight, and a straightedge held across the tops of the feet should line up with both feet (Fig. 63). Continue adjusting them until they are perfectly level.

Handsaw

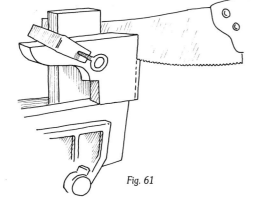

Fig. 61

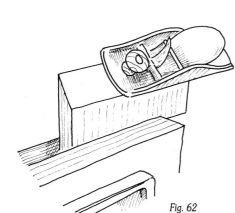

Fig. 62

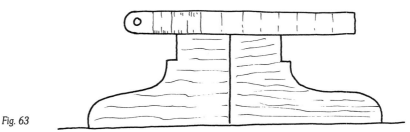

Fig. 63

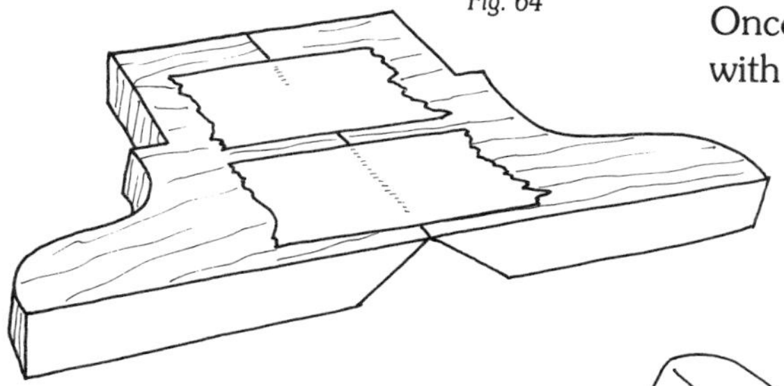

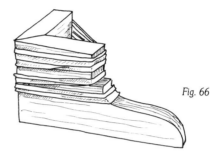

Fig. 64

Fig. 65

Fig. 66

GLUING THE FEET

Once the feet can be lined up as described above, lay them out with the mitre edges touching. Tape the pairs together with masking tape (Fig. 64). Turn them over and run glue into the mitres (Fig. 65). Close the feet together. The tape acts as a hinge and holds the feet in alignment. Slip some strong elastic bands over the feet to hold them in place while the glue sets (Fig. 66).

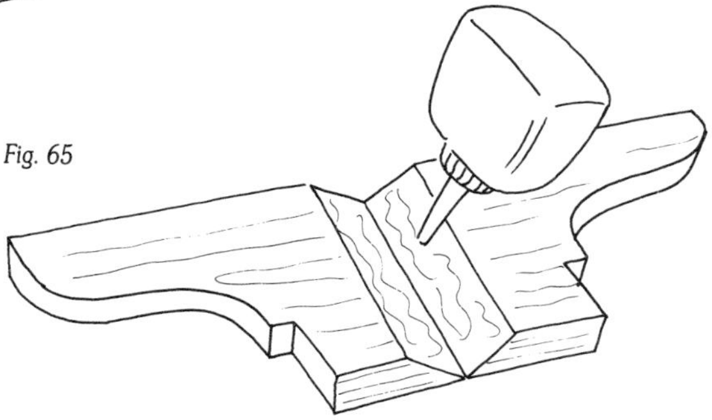

Fig. 67

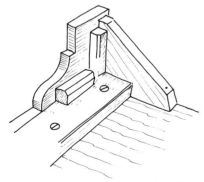

Fig. 68

FITTING THE FEET

Hold the feet in position against the bottom edge of the base moulding and trim the moulding with a shoulder plane until the feet fit neatly.

The feet are screwed and glued into the base moulding. Once you have achieved a good fit, select some large screws – 2¼in (56mm) gauge 10 – and drill a pilot hole through the feet (Fig. 67). Place the feet in position and hold them firmly either with masking tape or with a panel pin driven through each foot. Continue the pilot hole into the moulding to the full depth of the screw you are going to use. Repeat with the other face of the foot and the other three feet.

Change the drill bit, bore the shank holes for the screws and countersink the tops. Remove the feet, clean away the shavings from the underside of the feet and glue and screw the two front feet in place.

The back feet are screwed and glued in a similar manner after the back bracket has been fitted. The brackets at the back are usually pine, and they fit against the bottom board and are nailed to the bottom board and the end of the sub-frame (Fig. 68). The vertical face rests against the inside face of the back

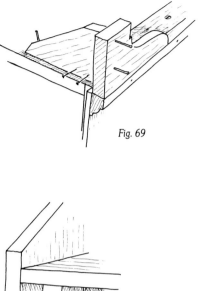

Fig. 69

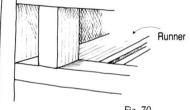

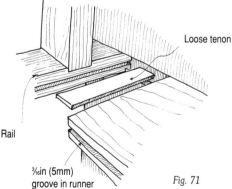

Runner

Fig. 70

foot, where it is glued. A couple of oval nails, driven in through the outside face of the bracket foot, hold it in position (Fig. 69).

When the glue is dry, fill the nail holes in the base moulding and in the back feet, and sandpaper them smooth. Do not round the edges of the moulding or the corners of the bracket feet.

Fitting the drawer runners

Make the drawer runners out of oak or some other hardwood. Saw them to size and plane them until they fit tightly in the housings cut into the sides of the bureau. The runners that support the top drawer also support the lopers, and they must, therefore, be twice as wide as the others (Fig. 70).

Cut them to length. At the front, they should butt accurately against the inside edge of the drawer rail. At the back, they should finish about ½in (12mm) from the edge of the back rebate.

When you have fitted the runners, cut a groove in the end of the runner to match the grooves cut in the front rail for the dust board. Saw out a small rectangle of ³⁄₁₆in (5mm) plywood, which will serve as a loose tenon, and press the runner in place (Fig. 71). Do the same for the other runners, and then cut the dust boards from some more of the ³⁄₁₆in (5mm) plywood. Fit the dust boards. When this is done, you can glue the runners to the sides. If they are at all loose, the dust boards will hold them in position.

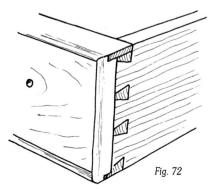

Fig. 72

Loose tenon

Rail

³⁄₁₆in (5mm)
groove in runner

Fig. 71

The drawers

The drawers are dovetailed together and are edged with cock beading (Fig. 72). You will have had some practice at dovetailing already, and if you cannot bear the thought of cutting more dovetails, rebate the fronts of the drawers, and either screw and glue, or nail the sides in position. If you nail them, punch the nail heads well below the surface of the sides after the glue is dry and before you rout the rebates for the cock beading.

If you need some persuasion to cut dovetails for the drawers, bear in mind that cutting dovetails in thin drawer sides is easy and quick because you can cut both sets at once, and the recesses for the dovetails, which are chopped out in the sides of the drawer, are only shallow.

MAKING THE DRAWER FRONTS

Saw and plane up the drawer fronts first. Start by fitting the largest drawer, which is at the bottom, so that if you make a mess of fitting it, you can use it for the next drawer up.

First, plane the edges until the drawer front can be slid into the drawer space, and then trim the ends until the board just fits.

Repeat with the other drawer fronts.

MAKING THE SIDES AND BACK

Select wood for the sides and back. Oak is ideal, but almost any wood will do. You could use ⅜in (9mm) plywood, but I would feel I had to conceal the top edge of the plywood with a strip of solid wood, and that takes time. (For advice on doing this see page 112.)

Cut and trim the edges of the side planks until they can be slid along the runners, and plane the front edge so that it is parallel with the edge of the bureau. While you are doing this, it is worth checking whether the edge facing the front of the bureau is at right-angles to the bottom edge. If both side planks are similar, there is no reason you cannot tack the two planks together and mark and cut the dovetails in one operation. If they are at slightly different angles, they will have to be cut separately.

GROOVING THE SIDES AND FRONT

Fit a ¼in (6mm) router bit into the router, set the router in its stand, and cut the grooves for the drawer bottoms. The groove in the sides is set ⅜in (9mm) up from the bottom edge and is ¼in (6mm) deep. The groove in the front is ⅜in (9mm) up and ⅜in (9mm) deep. Groove all the sides, making sure that you groove the inside faces and not the outside faces.

MARKING AND CUTTING THE DOVETAILS

Cut the dovetails on the bottom drawer first. These will take the longest, because the drawer is deeper. As you get quicker in the jointing, and the drawers get narrower as you work up, the work will progress at an encouraging rate. With a little practice you should be able to cut a row of lapped dovetails in less than an hour.

Take the two sides, place them together, insides touching, and line up the bottom edges and the front ends. When you have them lined up, hold them and tack them together with a pair of panel or veneer pins (Fig. 73).

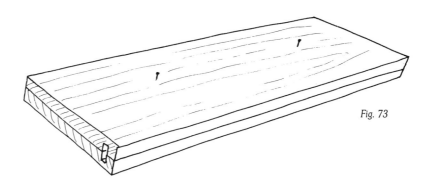

Fig. 73

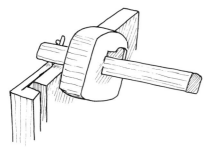

Fig. 74

Take your cutting gauge to mark the lap-line. Adjust it so that when you hold it against the inside face of the drawer front, the knife is just level with the bottom of the drawer groove (Fig. 74). If the dovetails do not cover this groove, there will be a hole in the side of the drawer.

When you have set the gauge, scribe the lap-line on the drawer front and, keeping the same setting, the shoulder-line for the dovetails on the drawer ends (Fig. 75).

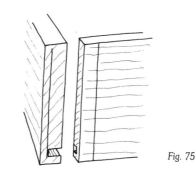

Fig. 75

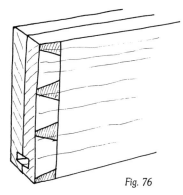

Fig. 76

Pencil in on one side the dovetail pattern you want to cut. Each dovetail should be approximately the same width, and the bottom one should conceal the groove in the drawer front (Fig. 76). You can tell where this is, because there is a groove in the sides at the same height.

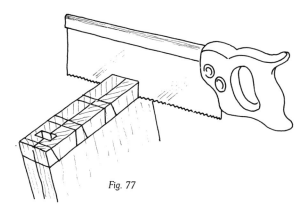

Fig. 77

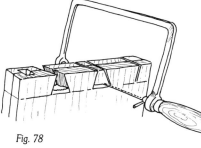

Fig. 78

Square across the ends with a set square and saw the dovetails (Fig. 77). Remove the waste with a coping saw (Fig. 78), then chisel the waste back to the shoulder-line (Fig. 79). Saw the ends (Fig. 80).

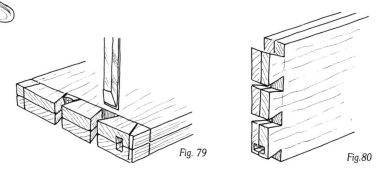

Fig. 79

Fig.80

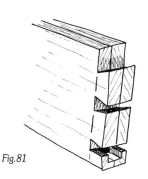

Fig.81

Before you separate the two sides, cut the back dovetails. These are simple through dovetails – two per side is enough – and because the backboard sits on the bottom of the drawer, the dovetails start above the groove (Fig. 81).

Separate the two sides and use the cutting gauge to scribe the shoulders on the inside of the sides (Fig. 82). Trim those shoulder-lines where you have not cut back quite far enough.

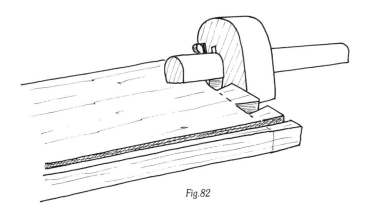

Fig.82

Lap

Shoulder

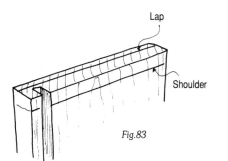

Fig.83

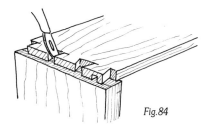

Fig.84

CUTTING THE PINS

This has been described in some detail already (see pages 85–7). The order of cutting is as follows.

Mark the lap-line on the edges of the drawer front (Fig. 83). Mark the inside shoulder-line – 3/8in (9mm) or equivalent to the thickness of the sides – with a marking gauge or a different, easily identifiable cutting gauge. Place the side over the front and align the joint. Nudge the tails a little way towards the front of the drawer. Use a knife or narrow saw to mark the edges of the dovetails (Fig. 84).

Lift the front in the vice a little way, rest the dovetail saw in the line and saw down the sides of the knife mark and inwards, stopping at the lap-line (Fig. 85).

Chop out the waste, stopping well before the chisel reaches the lap-line (Fig. 86).

Lift the front into the vice and clean up the pins, using a bevel-edged chisel and a knife or flat chisel, ground to about 45 degrees (Fig. 87).

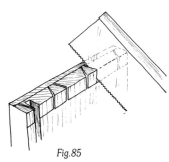

Fig.85

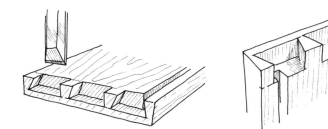

Fig.86

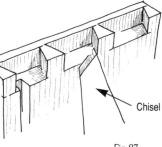

Chisel

Fig.87

Trim the inside edges of each dovetail, and then, supporting the row of tails with a batten, tap them into place.

FAULTS

Dovetails that are too loose may be caused by:
- Inaccurate marking;

- A saw that is too big or that is cutting with too much set or that has blunt teeth;

- Failure to nudge them across far enough;

- Failure to cut them square (when viewed from the end).

Dovetails that are too tight may be caused by:
- Inaccurate marking;

- Nudging the side too far;

- Failure to saw the pins vertically.

If there are gaps at the lap-line:
- Check the trimming of the recesses of the slots. The chisel work often slopes, because of variations in the grain, and this must be corrected.

- Check that the ends of the tails are at right angles to the sides.

CUTTING THE PINS AT THE BACK OF THE DRAWER

Fit the backboards for each drawer. Mark on each board its inside face and plane a radius along the top edge, so that it is easily identifiable.

Position the end board in the vice, outside outwards, and place the side over the end (Fig. 88). Nudge the side a little past the shoulder-line and mark the end-grain of the back plank with

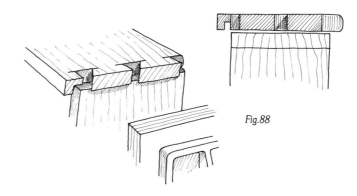

Fig.88

a knife. Mark the shoulders on the end plank and saw down the pins. Remove the waste with a coping saw and trim back to the shoulder-line (Figs. 89–91). Fit the dovetails (Fig. 92).

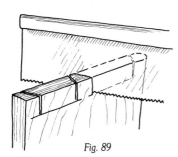

Fig. 89

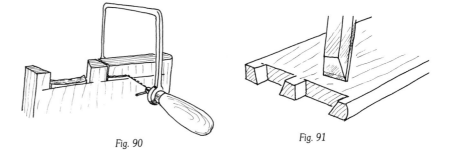

Fig. 90

Fig. 91

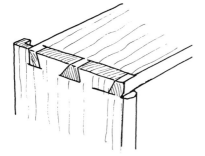

Fig. 92

When all the dovetails have been cut, and the drawers are ready for final assembly, dismantle the drawers, one at a time, and sand the inside surfaces clean. Plane a radius on the top edges of the sides and very carefully saw off from the top of each drawer the thickness of the cock beading (Fig. 93).

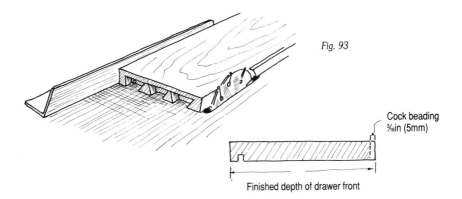

Fig. 93

Cock beading
³⁄₁₆in (5mm)

Finished depth of drawer front

The beading can be as large as you choose, but it does not need to be much thicker than ³⁄₁₆in (5mm), although if it is much thinner than that it will be flimsy. You only have to cut a strip from the top of the drawers – nowhere else. The rest is done when the drawers have been glued together, and you might be relieved to know that when the beading is fitted it will conceal much of your excellent dovetailing.

Cut out the drawer bottoms. Make them a good, smooth fit and then glue the drawers together. They will look wrong now because the sides are higher than the front, but that will change when the beading is in place.

The joints will look tighter if you clamp them while the glue dries. Arrange the clamps as shown in Fig. 94. Fit the bottom inside the drawer groove before clamping and hold it to the back of the drawer with a couple of tacks before applying pressure. The bottom should hold the sides square.

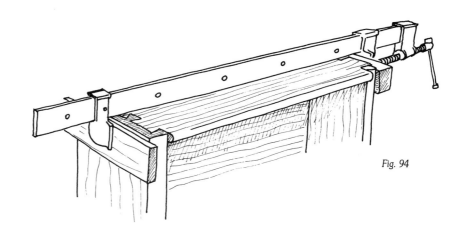

Fig. 94

Fig. 95

DRAWER SLIDES

Cut strips of hardwood and glue them to the underside of the drawers to reinforce and increase the surface area of the drawer that slides on the runners. Plane them flush with the sides of the drawers when the glue has dried (Fig. 95).

Fitting the lopers

The lopers slide into the spaces beside the dividers and the sides of the bureau, and they support the fall when the desk is opened. They should be made of straight-grained hardwood and need to slide easily. Their width is a fraction less than the space available, and, because a baize strip will be glued along the top edges, a height of 3/32–1/8in (3–4mm) less than the height available is about right (Fig. 96).

Cut the lopers to fit and plane them smooth. Plane the sawn-off front end smooth. This is capped by a small slip of wood ½in (12mm) thick (Fig. 97). Select a suitable pair of slips and glue

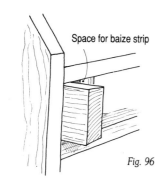

Space for baize strip

Fig. 96

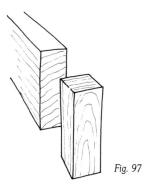

Fig. 97

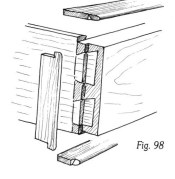

Fig. 98

them to the ends of the lopers, holding them in place with masking tape. Smooth the face and plane the edges and sides flush with the lopers.

Press a loper in position so that its front is level with the front of the bureau. Check at the back of the bureau. The loper should extend back almost to the rebate. If it is too long, trim it at the back. Round off the ends at the back.

Cock beading

The cock beading is fitted using very simple joints (Fig. 98). The top bead covers the full width of the drawer front. The side and bottom beads are set in rebates worked in the edges of the drawer, with a short mitre at the corners, and the remaining two-thirds of the bead is lapped as shown. Joints in the cock beading are made at right angles (Fig. 99).

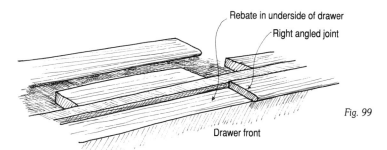

Rebate in underside of drawer

Right angled joint

Drawer front

Fig. 99

MAKING THE COCK BEADING

Choose some straight-grained, knot-free wood for the beading. It should be the same wood as that used for the carcass and drawer fronts. Plane the wood straight and square. The beading is moulded on the edge of the stick (Fig. 100), so saw the stick to the thickness of the drawer fronts plus the height of the cock bead above the drawer fronts.

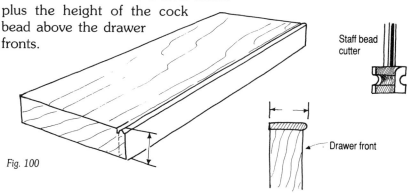

Staff bead cutter

Drawer front

Fig. 100

Take a ³⁄₃₂in (2mm) radius staff bead cutter, set this in the router and adjust its height so that the top of the bead is level with the top edge of the radius. With a bead as small as this, a satisfactory finish can be achieved with a single pass. After you have made each length of bead, cut it off with the circular saw and smooth the edge before moulding the next one.

Make plenty of beading. The lopers will need beads around the edges, as will all the drawers.

CUTTING THE REBATE FOR THE COCK BEADING

Fit a ³⁄₈in (9mm) or ½in (12mm) router bit and adjust the fence so that the router can cut a rebate at the sides and bottoms of the drawers. Set the depth stop of ³⁄₁₆in (5mm) or the thickness of the beading and the fence to a fraction over ³⁄₈in (9mm) (Fig. 101). Rout the sides of the drawers first, cutting each rebate in several stages. When the rebates at the sides are finished, rout the grooves on the bottom edges of the drawers.

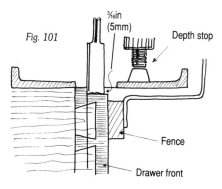

Fig. 101

³⁄₁₆in (5mm)

Depth stop

Fence

Drawer front

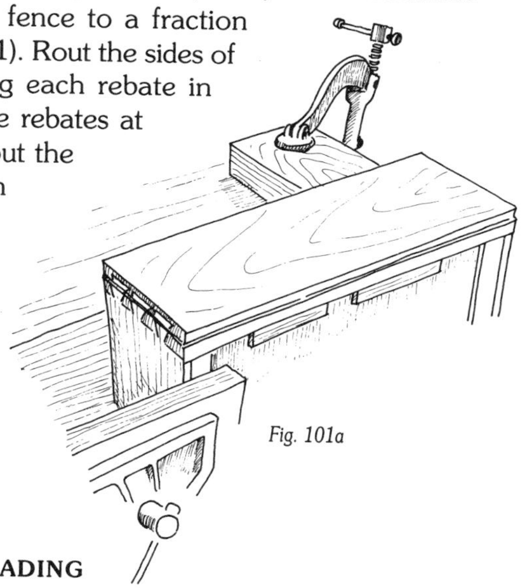

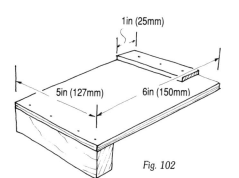

1in (25mm)

5in (127mm)   6in (150mm)

Fig. 102

Fig. 101a

FITTING THE COCK BEADING

The cock beading is glued into position. Hold it in place with masking tape until the glue has dried.

Fit the beading to the top edge of the top drawer first. I find the best way to hold the drawer is to grip its side in the vice and to support the other end of the drawer with a heavy block of wood, which rests on the bench. I use a hold-fast to secure the block and to prevent the drawer front from tipping sideways (Fig. 101a).

Choose a flat board on to which you can chop the mitres, and you might find it worthwhile making a small, neat bench hook to hold the beading while you are cutting it with the tenon saw (Fig. 102). Cut the top bead just a fraction longer than

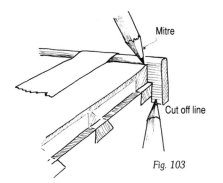

Fig. 103

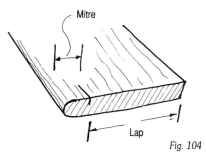

Fig. 104

necessary and place it on the top edge. Hold it there with masking tape wrapping it at the ends, but leaving the corners of the front visible. Mark the corners on the beading as shown in Fig. 103, and mark off its overall length.

Set a marking gauge to a fraction more than the depth of the bead. Make a mark at each end of the bead, to show where the mitre finishes and the lap joint begins (Fig. 104). This will be a constant measurement for all the joints, and you need to make the mitre joint big enough to see easily when you cut it. Remove the beading, cut it to length and slice off the mitres with a chisel. You will soon get used to estimating a 45 degree cut, and with a mitre as short as this, inaccuracies can easily be accommodated and should not be noticeable (Fig. 105).

When you have trimmed both ends, place the bead back on the edge of the drawer front and fit the first side piece. This is easy. First scribe a mark showing the depth of the mitre cut that has to be made, then use a set square to square across the end to give the depth of the lap you have to cut. The end of the bead should look as is shown in Fig. 106.

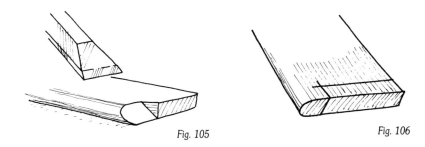

Fig. 105   Fig. 106

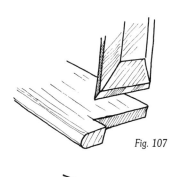

Fig. 107

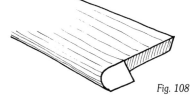

Fig. 108

Now chop off the lap with a sharp chisel held vertically (Fig. 107). This will probably take a couple of slices to reach the cut-off line. A final slice will chop out the mitre, and you can try it for fit (Fig. 108). It sounds easy, and once you have done one or two, you will find that it is.

Continue around the drawer, fitting the furthest side last. When all four beads are fitted, remove the top bead (leaving the others in position), run glue on the top edge and strap the bead down with strips of masking tape. Remove the side bead and glue it, then the bottom bead, and finally the bead on the opposite side. By removing only one bead at a time and fixing it before moving on to the next, you are less likely to experience problems in positioning the beads.

Try to be economical with the glue, sliding the beading into position in such a way that glue is not dragged over the front face of the drawer. Wipe away any drips that you see before leaving the glue to dry.

Drawer guides

The three lower drawers should all run smoothly. They are guided by the sides of the carcass, and if they rub or jam, you will have to plane or file away high spots inside the carcass.

The top drawer will need guides, however. Saw out the guides and plane them to the exact thickness of the dividers that separate the lopers from the drawer. Cut the front end of each guide square and scallop the other end (Fig. 109). Put it in position, parallel with the loper, which you should leave in place. Press it hard up against the divider at the front and hold it at the back with a clamp. Trim a short piece of stick to length and wedge it at the front to hold the guide in place (Fig. 110). Fit the second guide in the same way.

Try out the top drawer. It should slide in easily, as should both lopers. Adjust the position of the guide until all move freely and the drawer lies parallel to, and flush with, the front rails when it is pushed home.

Use a pencil to mark the position for each guide. Remove them one at a time, drill and countersink the scallop and fit them, this time gluing the front end (which butts against the divider) and on the underside to hold it to the runner. When you have made sure that it is in exactly the right place, drill and screw it from the back, and press the front end down again with the wedged stick.

Fitting out the interior of the bureau

The pigeon-holes and drawers built into the interior of the bureau are actually built inside a thin wooden framework (Fig. 111). This makes fitting out an easy and separate operation from the relatively heavy work of making the carcass and drawers, and it also means that the exact shape and style of the interior can be left undecided until the bureau is almost finished. A practical advantage of the thin surrounding box is that the drawers nestling beneath the pigeon-holes are raised slightly above the level of the shelf and will not become jammed by papers and pins rolling beneath them.

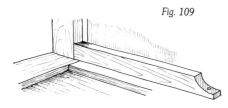

Fig. 109

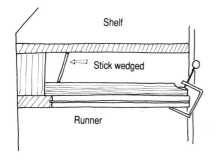

Shelf

Stick wedged

Runner

Fig. 110

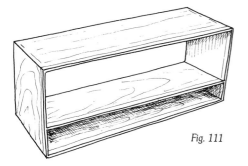

Fig. 111

The instructions given here relate to the design illustrated in the plans and shown in the photographs. Country-made bureaux tend to have a simpler style of interior than that seen in metropolitan pieces, and if you prefer, you can choose your own design, based on illustrations in country life magazines or furniture sale catalogues.

Traditionally, the interior fittings of a bureau conceal drawers, alcoves and hiding places. There are plenty of these in the piece illustrated, and you must use your own ingenuity to fit your own into the bureau you are making. Because all the woodworking takes place inside a flimsy outer shell, there is plenty of scope for false backs, lowered ceilings and hidden nests of drawers.

Making the outer shell

The shell and all the divisions making up the interior of this bureau are made principally from ¼in (6mm) plywood, the front edge of which is capped by a strip of cherry wood measuring ¾ × ¼in (20 × 6mm) (Fig. 112). Make up your capping pieces a fraction wider than the ¼in (6mm) plywood and cut out all the components for the interior. Glue on the capping as shown in Fig. 113. Make sure that when each piece is glued on there is no perceptible tilt. Hold the capping with masking tape, and when the glue has dried, trim the capping smooth and flush with a shoulder plane.

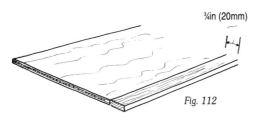

¾in (20mm)

Fig. 112

Masking tape

Fig. 113

MARKING OUT THE SHELL

The shell is fitted and inserted from the back of the bureau. Its four corners are dovetailed together. You will need two side pieces, a top and bottom. They are all the same width, and you must trim the ends so that each one can be slid in from the back (Fig. 114). When each piece is a close sliding fit, you can mark out the position of each joint.

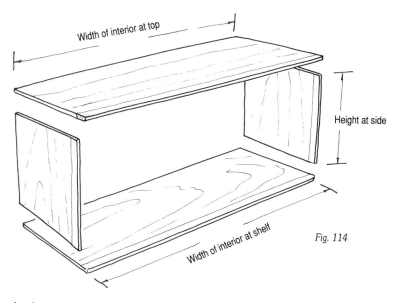

Fig. 114

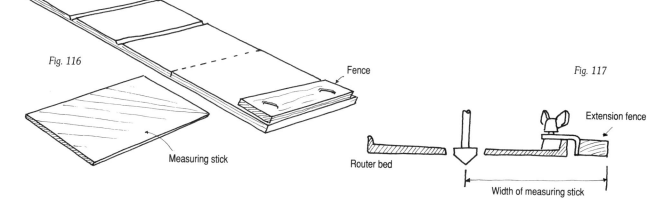

Fig. 115

Simple through dovetails are used at the corners, and the facing edge can be mitred as shown in Fig. 115. When you are designing the dovetail pins, make them at least 1in (25mm) wide, because narrow ones are vulnerable and likely to snap off. (Instructions for cutting through dovetails can be found on page 12.) When the dovetails are finished, cut and fit the shelf and the divisions for the pigeon-holes.

The shelf above the drawers and the divisions making the pigeon-holes slide into V-shaped grooves. These can be cut with a chisel and smoothed with a rebate plane, or very quickly routed using a chamfer 45 degree V cutter, with the extension fence fitted into the router. The groove is at right angles to the front face of the components, and it is cut to half its thickness – i.e., ⅛in (4mm). Figs. 116 and 117 show the minimal marking out that is required and a suitable fence arrangement to enable these grooves to be cut quickly.

Fig. 116

Fig. 117

For those who prefer to cut the grooves by hand, the easiest way I have found is as follows. Mark out the centre and edges of each groove with a set square and marking knife. Take the tenon saw and, down the centre mark, make a fine cut to slightly less than half the thickness of the board. Use a sharp chisel, which is held at 45 degrees, to cut away the waste and finish off with the edge of a rebate plane.

The pieces that slide into the grooves have to be cut accurately to length – i.e., the distance between boards plus ¼in (6mm) – and are then quickly trimmed to fit with a sharp plane.

When all the grooves have been cut, assemble the dovetail joints, insert the shelf and dividers and then slide the whole unit into the bureau. If it is difficult doing this, remove the shelf and dividers. If it will still not slide in, you must inspect the fit of the shell very carefully and you may have to trim back some of the shoulders of the dovetails and pins. When you have achieved a satisfactory fit, glue the joints together and insert the shell.

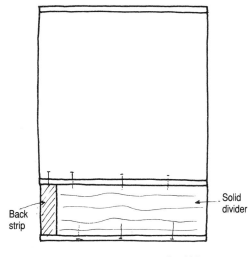

Back strip

Solid divider

Fig. 118

THE DRAWERS

Fit and glue the spacer planks between the shelf and the bottom board which separate the drawers and support the back edge of the shelf (Figs. 118 and 119). Then cut and fit the drawer fronts, sides and backs.

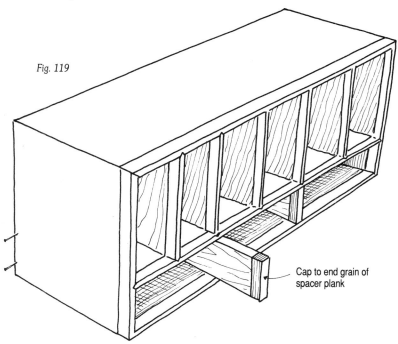

Fig. 119

Cap to end grain of spacer plank

Fig. 120

Use the router, set in the router stand, to rout a rebate in the bottom edges of the sides and fronts of the drawers. The rebate in the front should be a little deeper than those in the sides.

The drawers are dovetailed together, and because the work is so fine and the distance covered by the dovetails so small, you can cut down on the size of the pins, until they taper to the thickness of a saw cut (Fig. 120).

Instructions for cutting lapped dovetails and through dovetails are given on pages 12 and 81. The method of cutting the fine lapped dovetails is exactly the same as for the dovetails in the drawer fronts of the main drawers, except that there is only a single entry point for each pin when you use the dovetail saw.

SECRET DRAWERS

It is customary to include various secret compartments and hiding holes in a bureau such as this. Usually the maker will conceal at least some compartments behind the aprons fitted between the sides of the pigeon-holes, which become drawer fronts. There is also scope at the back of the pigeon-holes to include storage space, concealed behind a false panel. The drawers beneath the shelf can have false bottoms, or you can fit thin boxes into the space behind the drawers before cutting and fitting the drawer sides.

Devise some subtle schemes of your own and incorporate them into the bureau.

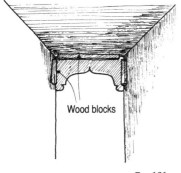

Wood blocks

Fig. 121

CUTTING AND FITTING THE APRONS

Design a suitable profile for the apron. Choose some planed-up and straight-grained wood and cut it into short lengths to fit precisely into the spaces between the dividers. You can take fine shavings from the end-grain of the aprons if you use a sharp shoulder plane and a simple shooting board.

Draw the design on the front face of the apron and use a fret saw to cut the pattern. (See pages 149–150 for use of the fret saw.)

Where appropriate, glue the aprons into position and support them on the inside with narrow wood blocks (see Fig. 121).

Making the fall

Fetch the wood you have put aside for the fall, plane it smooth and thickness it.

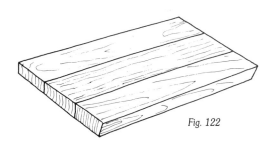

Fig. 122

The fall is made in two stages. The central section is made first, and this is simply a matter of shooting the joints and gluing the planks together (Fig. 122).

When the central section is glued, plane one face smooth and trim the top edge, then the two sides. Then finish the top edge again, so that all three sides are straight and square.

Now plane up the three rim pieces. Make them longer than necessary and a little wider than required to give some latitude for error. Saw the mitres at the ends of the two side pieces and trim them exactly square with the shoulder plane before cutting and trimming the first end of the top piece.

Lay the fall flat on the bench and check the accuracy of your work (Fig. 123). Correct any errors before marking and cutting the mitre at the other end. By now you should have had some practice at this, and it should all go swimmingly. If you have problems and cut back the top piece too much for the mitres ever to fit, you can still trim back the edge of the inner board a little and use up the extra width that you included as a precautionary measure when sawing out the rim pieces.

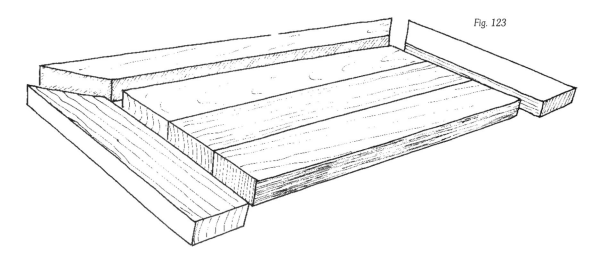

Fig. 123

When you lay the fall flat on the bench, the rim pieces should nestle into place, with no gaps, and there should be no need to hold them in position. The joints between the planks of the central section were straight shot joints, but between the rim pieces and the central section and in the mitres themselves, you need a loose tongue that will permit movement between the boards and, to a limited extent, prevent warping.

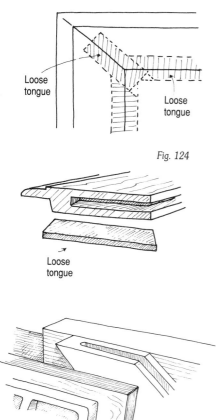

Fig. 124

Loose
tongue

Loose
tongue

Loose
tongue

Fig. 125

Cut some straight-grained hardwood to make the loose tongue. It should be about 1in (25mm) wide and ¼in (6mm) thick. You can now plan the positions for the loose tongues in the mitres. They should stop just short of the rebate that is cut in the edge of the fall (Fig. 124). You do not want the mechanics of the joint to be exposed by the rebate.

Place a ¼in (6mm) straight cutter in the router and fit the parallel fence, with a short batten fitted to it. Pencil in the end marks for the grooves in the mitres. The edges of the fall planks are so narrow that it will be difficult to control the router. Increase the area by clamping the fall to a thick, parallel-sided plank, which is held in the vice, and rout the grooves in the sides and top edge of the central plank and in the inside edges of the rib pieces. Now tilt the rib pieces, mitre upwards, and rout them, too (Fig. 125).

Assemble the fall, with the tongues in place. Apply glue to the tongues and edges and clamp them up. Use the minimum possible force to prevent locking stresses into the fall, which might cause it to warp.

When the glue is dry, use a sharp plane, set to a fine cut, to plane one side flat. If the mouth of the plane is adjustable, set it to a minimum clearance. This will help prevent the blade from pulling up splintery shavings if you run into adverse grain. When you have flattened one side, square up around the edges of the rims and smooth the inside.

REBATING THE FALL

Hold the fall in place against the bureau. With any luck, it will lie nicely against the sloping sides. It probably will not do so, however, because by now you can expect the sides to have shrunk a little, and the slopes are quite likely to be slightly curved. Use a shoulder plane to flatten the slopes if they are a little high in the centre; otherwise leave them, because they are likely to need trimming before the fall is fully fitted.

Pencil on the edges of the fall the extent of the rebate required for the fall to fit easily between the sides. The rebate should not be more than about ⅜in (9mm), or the lip will become weak and vulnerable.

Pencil on the edges the depth of the rebate and then set a ½in (12mm) straight, two-flute cutter in the router, and fit a long – about 18in (460mm) – fence to the parallel fence attachment. The extra length makes the router a little easier to control at

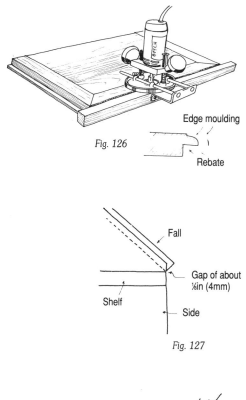

Fig. 126

Edge moulding

Rebate

Fall

Gap of about
⅙in (4mm)

Shelf

Side

Fig. 127

corners. Clamp the fall to a trestle and, working on one side at a time, rout out the rebate (Fig. 126).

While you still have the router out and the parallel fence attached, fit a rounding-over cutter in the router. Test the setting on some scrap wood, then rout around the face side of the three rims. The bottom edge does not require a moulding.

Fitting the hinges

You will need two heavy brass back flap hinges for the fall. They are recessed into the front edge of the writing shelf and into the inside face of the fall. Before they can be fitted, the fall must be fitted so that when it lies against the sloping sides of the bureau, the bottom corner of the fall is almost touching the writing shelf (Fig. 127). At the moment, this is unlikely to be the case, and so first you must mark the slope and carefully plane away its sides until the fall fits.

When you have done this, place the fall in position and check to see how the top lip of the fall rests against the bureau top. There may need to be some trimming here as well.

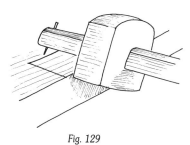

Fig. 128

MARKING

Pull out the lopers, cover them with a piece of thick cloth and let the fall rest on them. Place the hinges in position, with the axis of each in the centre of the gap between the fall and writing shelf, and mark around the hinges with a knife or sharp hard pencil (Fig. 128).

Remove the fall and cut out the recesses for the hinges. You will need to mark the depth of the hinge with a marking gauge and saw down both sides of each hinge before cutting out the waste with a sharp chisel. Figs. 129–133 show the order in which the work is carried out.

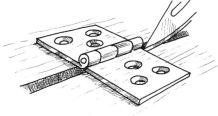

Fig. 129

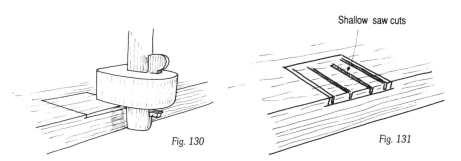

Fig. 130

Shallow saw cuts

Fig. 131

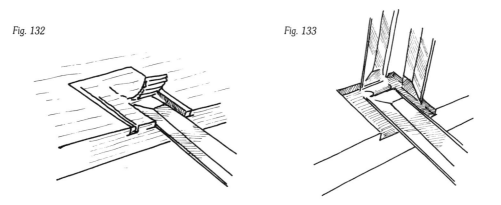

Fig. 132   Fig. 133

When the recesses in the fall are ready, insert the hinges, which should fit tightly, and if necessary hold them with a single screw. Check the positioning on the writing shelf before cutting the second set of recesses.

Screw the hinges to the writing shelf and make any necessary adjustments to the rebate or the positioning of the hinges until the fall fits perfectly.

Drawer stops

Press each drawer into place. The cock beading at the edges of each drawer should be flush with the sides of the bureau. When each one is in position, look behind the bureau to see if any of the drawer bottoms extend beyond the rebate in the sides. If they do, they will need to be trimmed. Glue and tack wooden blocks to the ends of the runners, to stop the drawers being pushed in too far.

The back

Replace the ¼in (6mm) plywood back. Hold it in position and nail it with flat-headed wire nails.

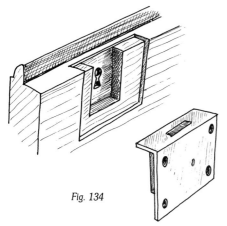

Fig. 134

Fitting the lock

Fit the lock to the inside top face of the fall. Locks vary, but it is usually worthwhile making a simple cardboard template of the inner casing of the lock, with the keyhole cut in it, to simplify marking out. The facing plate of the lock is recessed by its own thickness, and the edge plate that encloses the locking bar is also recessed into the top edge of the bureau (Fig. 134).

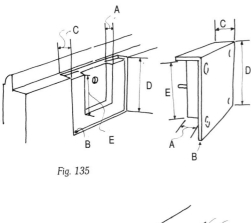

Fig. 135

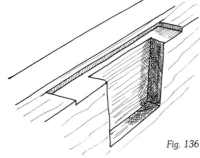

Fig. 136

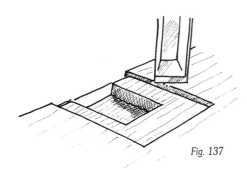

Fig. 137

Pencil in the outline of the facing plate and the outline of the inner case on the inside of the fall (Fig. 135). Rout out or chisel out the recess for the inner casing. Cut the shallow recess at the edge for the top edge of the lock (Fig. 136).

Mark and drill an undersize hole for the keyhole, but do not shape the keyhole just yet.

Position the lock in the recess, pressing it down hard against top edge. Use a knife to incise around the edge of the facing plate and then chisel out the shallow recess for the face plate. Do this cleanly by working to a chiselled line about ¹⁄₁₆in (1.5mm) from the incised line, and then, when the recess is smoothed and all but finished, chop the edge back to the incised line (Fig. 137).

Press the lock into position. Adjust the position of the keyhole if necessary, and then mark out its shape and cut it out with a fret saw. Screw the lock in position. Dab some white PVA glue on the locking bar and shut the fall. Turn the key to press the bar against the edge of the bureau top.

Open the bureau and define the mark left by the locking bar with a pencil. Cut out a thin, shallow mortice for the lock.

Remove the lock and the fall and store the hinges safely until you need them after finishing the bureau.

Fitting the handles

Brass pear drops are fitted to the drawers by a single bolt, which passes through the drawer front. The position of the drops is marked on the plans. Note that they are all set a fraction above the centre line of the drawers.

Remove the drops once you have them fitted, and replace them after the bureau has been stained and polished, but before it is waxed.

FINISHING

Smoothing

Use a cabinet scraper to remove all signs of coarse sandpaper and belt sanding marks, before finishing the bureau with 220 grit open cut paper. An orbital sander is ideal for this work, and it will reach into most of the spaces, but take care when you are sanding the drawer fronts, because the orbital action can hammer the cock beading and splinter it.

Fill any holes, nail heads and crevices with two-part wood filler, and when the filler is set, sand those areas very carefully. You must not leave any surplus filler in the grain next to the hole.

Staining

The bureau in the photograph was fumed in ammonia gas before staining. The fuming enables quite a dramatic colour change to be achieved without dirtying the grain by piling on a lot of stain. The procedure for fuming is described on page 50. Cherry wood needed a pre-fume treatment of dilute tannic acid before it was sealed into the clear polythene bag with the ammonia saucers left in the drawers, writing shelf and on the floor at the front of the bureau.

The fuming process was carefully monitored to make sure that the gas coloured the wood evenly. This could be seen through the polythene, and it was sometimes necessary to cut a slit in the clear polythene in order move or replenish a saucer of the ammonia. After fuming, the bureau was left to stand for a few days before a thin coat of Canadian Cedar mixed with a little American Walnut was brushed over all the showing surfaces.

Polishing

Finish the bureau with brushed shellac, using either button polish for a bright, warm colour or garnet for a deeper brown. Three or four coats of shellac are sufficient, brushed on in the manner described on pages 62–3. If you want to use a grain filler, this should be used after the stain has dried and been sealed with a thin brush coat of shellac. Filler can be bought ready coloured, and it is applied across the grain with a cloth. Then wipe with a rough cloth to remove any surplus. Leave the filler to dry before applying shellac.

Waxing

Use a soft, slow-drying brown wax to finish, and apply a fresh coat of wax each week for a few months, until the bureau is a beautiful rich, soft brown.

COUCH WITH DRAWERS

The couch featured here is made from larch. It has a curved, panelled back and panelled sides, and beneath the seat are three drawers. It is upholstered with flame-retardant foam.

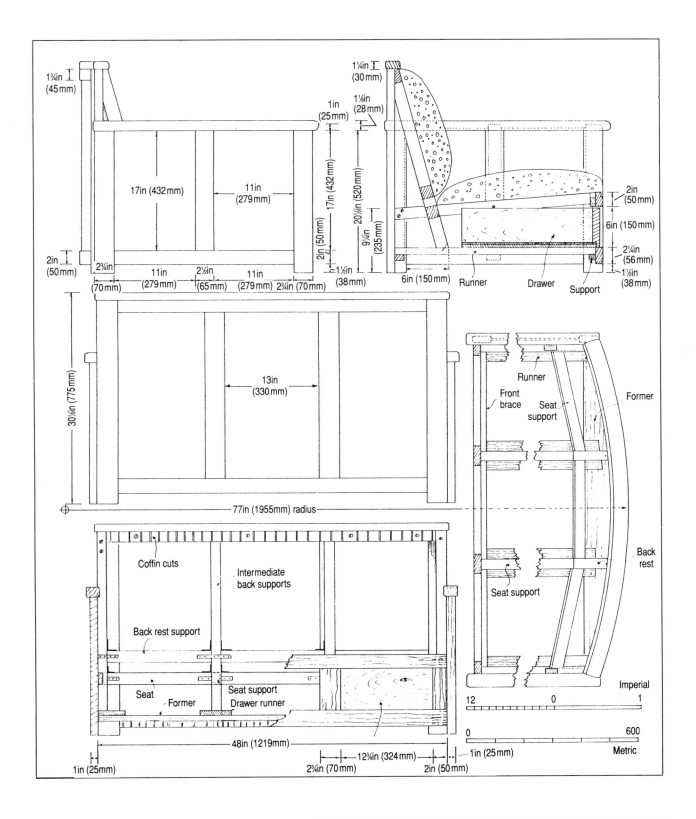

1¾in (45mm)

17in (432mm)

11in (279mm)

2in (50mm)

2¾in (70mm)

11in (279mm)

2½in (65mm)

11in (279mm)

2¾in (70mm)

1in (25mm)

17in (432mm)

2in (50mm)

1½in (38mm)

1¼in (30mm)

1⅛in (28mm)

20½in (520mm)

9¼in (235mm)

6in (150mm)

2in (50mm)

6in (150mm)

2¼in (56mm)

1½in (38mm)

Runner

Drawer

Support

13in (330mm)

30½in (775mm)

77in (1955mm) radius

Front brace

Runner

Seat support

Former

Back rest

Seat support

Coffin cuts

Intermediate back supports

Back rest support

Seat

Former

Seat support

Drawer runner

48in (1219mm)

1in (25mm)

2¾in (70mm)

12¾in (324mm)

2in (50mm)

1in (25mm)

Imperial

12

0

1

0

600

Metric

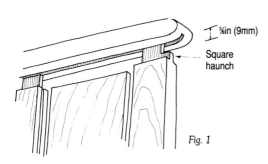

⊥ ⅜in (9mm)

Square
haunch

Fig. 1

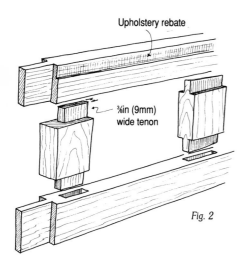

Upholstery rebate

⅜in (9mm)
wide tenon

Fig. 2

CONSTRUCTION

Make the sides first. The framework is grooved and joined with mortice and tenon joints. The inside edge of the framework and the underside of the armrest are grooved with a ¼in (6mm) wide groove to hold the panels. Since the tenons are also ¼in (6mm) wide, you can leave a square haunch at the outside edge of the tenons, to fill the gap in the joint left by the groove (Fig. 1).

Once you have made the end frames, fit them together, and glue the joints except for those holding the armrests, which are left unglued for the time being so that the panels can be fitted.

Cut out all the panels, including the back panels, and join them with a butt joint to make up the required width. Do not cut them exactly to width. Once the panels are joined, bring them into the house, and stack them neatly, with spacers between them to allow warm air to circulate. Leave them for as long as you can before trimming them to fit the framework.

Mortice together the front framework. This is not grooved, as the side and back panels are, so the joints are straightforward (Fig. 2). It can be glued together as soon as the joints are finished. Rout a rebate in the top edge for the upholstery.

The back panel

Although the back framework is curved, it is made up as a flat frame. It is then bent around a rigid former after the panels are inserted. You will need to make the rails of the back framework a little longer than those of the front. This is because the back loses width slightly as it is curved around the former. When the back framework is completed, fit the panels.

The larch panels in the settee featured in the photographs are ⅜in (9mm) thick, and they have to be bevelled on the inside to fit the ¼in (6mm) groove. Bevel panels with the grain, before tackling the cross-grain bevels at the ends.

Fit the panels and leave only the smallest room for expansion in the groove – ⅛in (4mm) overall is enough. Unless you are using exceptionally dry wood, the problem is one of shrinkage, which can easily be as much as ½in (12mm) over a 12in (300mm) panel.

When the panels are held in the back frame and you have glued the mortice and tenon joints holding the framework together, cut out the curved former and the top capping piece.

The illustration shows an economical way of obtaining both pieces from a single plank (Fig. 3). Cut a second former from any scrap timber, to keep the back symmetrical when it is bent.

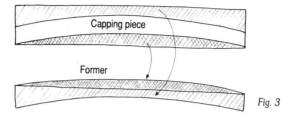

Fig. 3

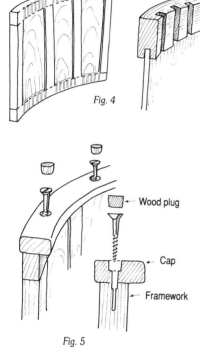

Fig. 4

Fig. 5

Although you may be lucky, I think you will find it is virtually impossible to bend the back against the formers. To get it to bend, you will have to make a series of coffin cuts part way through the top and bottom rails to weaken the frame (Fig. 4). Make the cuts on the inside of the framework, where they will be concealed by the upholstery.

Before nailing the lower rail to the former, run glue into the coffin cuts, and along the bottom former. If you are using the same large garden nails that you can see in the photograph, pre-drill the frame and former before nailing. Counterbore, then screw and glue the top capping piece in place (Fig. 5).

Insert the panels into the side frames, and glue and clamp down the armrests (Fig. 6).

Counterbore, and then glue and screw the settee framework together (Fig. 7). Fit a few temporary diagonals in position to hold the framework square and fit the drawer runners and guides.

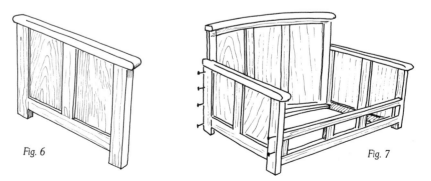

Fig. 6   *Fig. 7*

Fit the drawer fronts, the sides and the backs, and then use the circular saw or router to rebate the ends of the drawers to hold the sides. Groove the sides and fronts to hold the bottoms, and then assemble the drawers, gluing and nailing the sides into

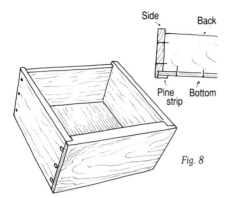

Side   Back

Pine   Bottom
strip

Fig. 8

the rebates at the front, and nailing the backs in place between the sides (Fig. 8). Drawers are opened by sliding a finger beneath the bottom rail of the seat and pulling on a fingerhold glued to the underside of the drawer. The illustration shows a very simple grip, made from plywood, which you can glue and tack close to the front of each drawer (Fig. 9).

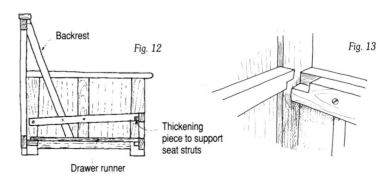

Fig. 9

A simple wooden framework supports the upholstery, and is screwed and glued in position as illustrated in Fig. 10.

The canted backrest supports are fitted first. These are screwed to the back and lie flush with the side frameworks, to which they are glued and screwed.. The armrests are notched to accommodate the supports. Fit a small infilling piece to fill the gap that shows between the support and the back stile (Fig. 11). Do the same on the other side.

Fit the seat support on each side. This is cross-halved with the back support and notched at the front framework to fit against a thickening piece measuring 2×1in (50×25mm), which is screwed to the top rail (Figs. 12 and 13).

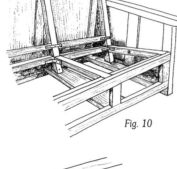

Fig. 10

Fig. 11

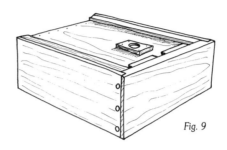

Backrest

Fig. 12

Fig. 13

Thickening
piece to support
seat struts

Drawer runner

Fit a beam just beneath the capping piece of the backrest . Once again this is persuaded to fit the curve of the back by making a series of coffin cuts, about 2in (50mm) apart and at least half-way through its thickness. Once you have planed the

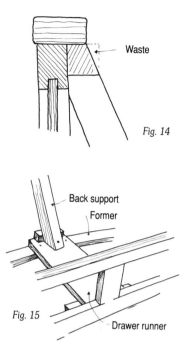

Waste

Fig. 14

Back support

Former

Fig. 15

Drawer runner

top and back edge to the appropriate angle, glue and screw it into the angle between the cap and the back rail (Fig. 14).

Now fit a couple of intermediate verticals between the end supports. Like the backrest supports at the ends, these are bevelled to fit against the back frame and tuck under the capping piece. They are centred on the centre stiles of the back panelling, and the bottom ends fit between or on the drawer runners, where they are screwed against a wood block, glued and nailed to the drawer runners (Fig. 15).

Two horizontal beams are fitted between the backrest supports. Because of the curve, the angles at which the ends are cut have to be measured with an angle gauge, and the beams themselves can either be cross-halved into the rests (Fig. 16) or butted and secured with screws and metal plates (Fig. 17).

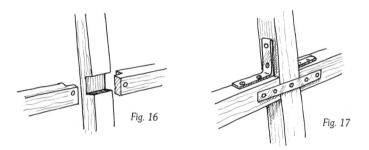

Fig. 16

Fig. 17

Although it is not necessary to have two beams at the back of the seat to stretch the upholstery against, it is actually easier if you do. Fit the lower (seat) support first, and when they are secured, fit the upper (backrest) supports, leaving a gap between the beams so that webbing and fabric can be passed between them (Fig. 18).

Apply two coats of wax polish to the settee.

Fig. 18

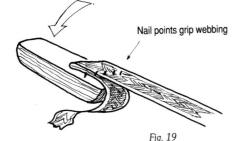

Nail points grip webbing

Fig. 19

Downwards pressure

Webbing

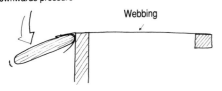

UPHOLSTERY

You will need webbing, hessian, upholstery foam and calico. You will also need some ⅝in(15mm) upholstery tacks and some ⅜in (9mm) tacks or a powerful staple gun. The webbing will have to be tensioned, so you will need a pair of grips as well. If you have not got any grippers, you can make the simple device illustrated in Fig. 19, which will work well.

Fit the webbing to the seat first. The webbing should be woven as shown in Fig. 20. I fitted the short runs first, and then the long ones, but if you are short of webbing, it would be sensible to cut the long ones first.

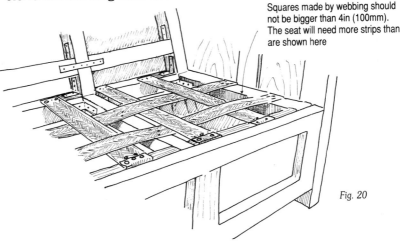

Squares made by webbing should not be bigger than 4in (100mm). The seat will need more strips than are shown here

Fig. 20

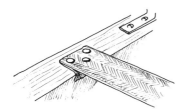

Fig. 21

Web tensioned

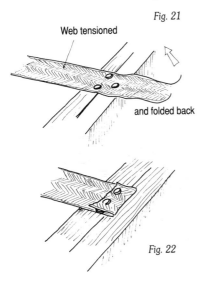

and folded back

Fig. 22

The webbing is fixed with ⅝in (15mm) upholstery tacks. Each length is folded under at one end and tacked in place (Fig. 21). It is tensioned and tacked with three tacks at the other end, then folded back and secured with two more tacks (Fig. 22). Plan ahead as you fit the webbing, because it is much easier to operate a tensioner in some positions than in others. Tension towards you when you are webbing the seat, and upwards when you are working on the backrest.

Weave the webbing at right angles to the first layer. Fix one end, tension the other and tack that end, too. Work from the back to the front of the seat, and upwards towards the top of the backrest.

When both the seat and backrest are webbed, cover the webbing with hessian. You will need one piece for the seat and one for the back, but only fit the seat piece at this stage. This

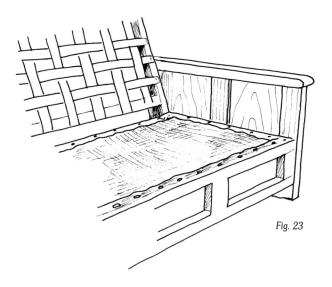

Fig. 23

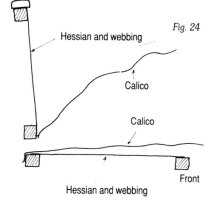

Fig. 24

Hessian and webbing

Calico

Calico

Front

Hessian and webbing

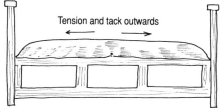

Tension and tack outwards

Fig. 25

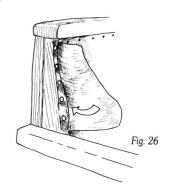

Fig. 26

should be stretched tight against the webbing. Fold the edge right round, and insert ³⁄₈in (9mm) tacks or ½in (12mm) staples at 1in (25mm) intervals all the way round (Fig. 23). Do not cover the space between the two bottom back rails.

Cut the foam to fit each seat. Before fitting it, cut the calico to fit over the foam, leaving enough to pull tight and fasten to the frame. When you have done this, slip the seating calico into the gap between the back rails, and staple or tack it from behind, by slipping your hand between the webbing.

When you have done this and before you insert the foam, fit the hessian over the backrest and fasten it all round. Also fasten the bottom edge of the calico (Fig. 24). It becomes very awkward to fasten them after the foam is fitted.

Insert the foam on the seat, holding it in place with some dabs of latex adhesive or double-sided adhesive tape, and draw the calico over it. Tension it and tack it at the centre first, then the centre of each side, and then, tensioning the calico as you go, work towards the corners (Fig. 25). The back is covered in the same way.

When this is done, cover the seat with the covering fabric. The fabric can be thrust between the back and seat, and held by two or three tacks. It is then drawn up to the edge of the capping piece of the backrest and forwards to the front edge of the settee, where it is tacked or stapled down. At the sides, you will have to cut small ear pieces that cover the side support and infilling (Fig. 26). Conceal the nail heads or staples with gimp, inserting nails every 4in (100mm) and gluing with latex glue.

HANGING MIRROR

This is a fairly simple Georgian wall mirror. The mirrored glass need not be bevelled at the edges and so is easy to obtain. The mirror consists of three units: the frame, which is stained a deep mahogany colour and gilded on the concave section of the moulding bordering the glass, and two extension pieces, which are wrapped around the frame at the top and bottom. These are veneered and stained a slightly lighter tone than the frame, before being polished to a high finish.

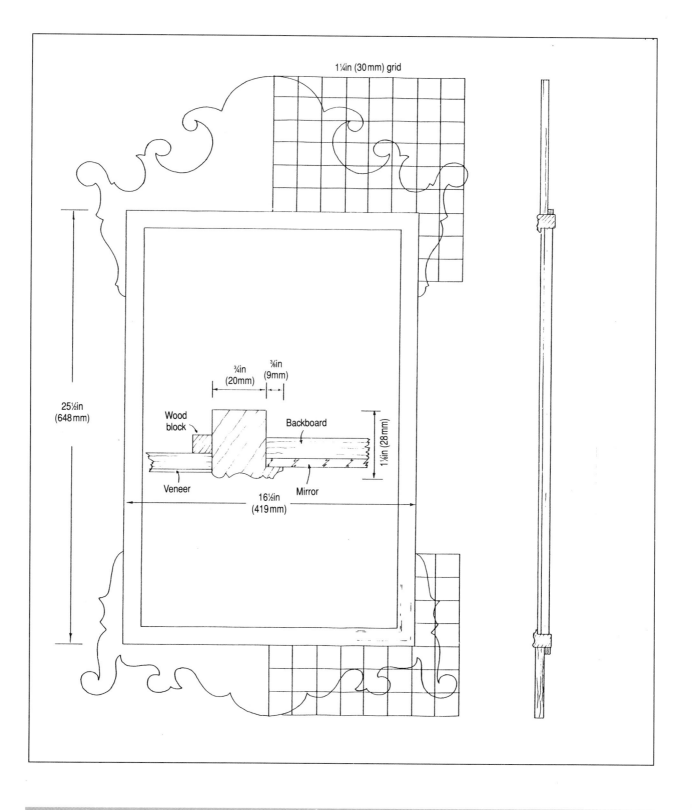

1¼in (30mm) grid

25½in
(648mm)

¾in
(20mm)

⅜in
(9mm)

Wood
block

Backboard

1⅛in (28mm)

Veneer

Mirror

16½in
(419mm)

CONSTRUCTION

Make the frame first. If you can find a suitable framing mould-ing that you can adapt to suit this project you will save yourself a lot of time. If you cannot, choose some straight-grained hard-wood of a suitable section and make the moulding yourself. This is not difficult, but it is a little time consuming.

I made the moulding for this mirror from some strips of Brazilian mahogany, 1⅛in (28mm) planed square, and I shaped the moulding with a home-made moulding tool.

First, I made the cutter, which I filed from a narrow plate of silver steel, which is obtainable from most tool shops. To make the blade, I stuck some masking tape on the steel and used a pen to draw the profile on the tape (Fig. 1). Next, with the plate held in the vice, with just enough poking above the jaws to work with, I filed the edge until it conformed with the line I had drawn (Fig. 2). When I had filed the shape perfectly, I moved the plate

Fig. 1

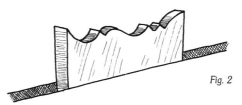

Fig. 2

sideways, until the shaped part was overhanging the end of the jaws. Then I filed a sharpening bevel on the back of the blade, to make a ragged and quite sharp cutter. I then sharpened this with finer, rat-tailed files, and finally sharpening stones until I had a sharp and smooth-edged cutter (Fig. 3).

The cutter is not used like a plane blade or chisel, but more like a scraper, so the last step is to roll a hook at the edge of the cutter, and to do this you need a burnishing tool or a smooth, hardened piece of steel. I used the back of a gouge and the shank of a masonry nail (Fig. 4).

The holder is made from two parts, clamped with bolts, and it is held with both hands and used like a spokeshave (Fig. 5). A temporary fence is tacked on to both sides of the blade, and the sole of the holder is planed at the angle shown in Fig. 6 to brace the cutter in its maximum cutting position. The sole on the leading edge is slightly curved to allow the cutter to be

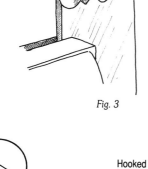

Fig. 3

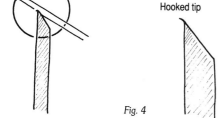

Hooked tip

Fig. 4

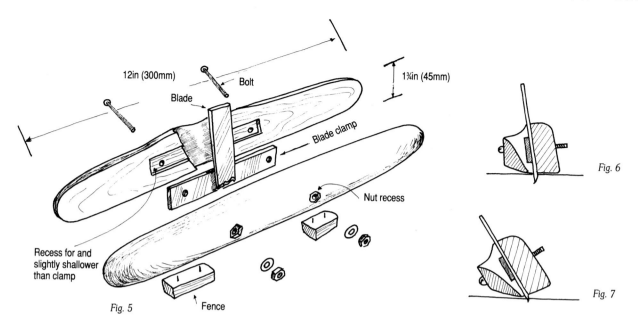

12in (300mm)

Bolt

Blade

1¾in (45mm)

Blade clamp

Nut recess

Recess for and
slightly shallower
than clamp

Fig. 5

Fence

Fig. 6

Fig. 7

rocked forward, limiting its bite (Fig. 7). With a little practice, you will find this a versatile and easy tool to use. Work on short lengths of moulding, working into the wood from one end of the moulding strip. Remember to keep the blade clear of shavings and try not to dig into the wood you are shaping – fine, frequent shavings will result in a more satisfactory moulding.

When you have made the moulding, cut it into the four pieces that make up the frame. Saw the mitres and glue them together. If you have difficulty sawing the mitres at 45 degrees, you might find the sawing jig illustrated in Fig. 8 helpful.

If you do not have a proper clamping jig for holding the frame while the glue dries, the device illustrated below, using picture wire and wood blocks will help (Fig.9).

When the frame is made, cut out the backing board that supports the glass, join it where necessary and fit it into the frame. Hold it in place temporarily with glue blocks. This will help to strengthen the frame while the extension pieces are fitted.

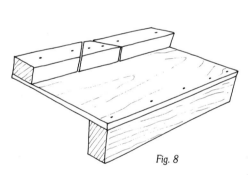

Fig. 8

Wood blocks pushed sideways
tensions wire and squeezes
corners

Fig. 9

Each extension piece is made from three pieces of wood, ⅜in (9mm) thick. Plywood is satisfactory, but I have used pine. Cut the extension pieces roughly to shape at this stage, then fit the main top piece against the top of the frame, leaving about ¹⁄₁₆in (1.5mm) at the edges overhanging the frame. Hold the top piece with three dowels, inserted and glued into the top, and located into ¼in (6mm) holes in the top of the frame (Fig. 10). Do not bring the piece too close to the front edge of the frame, because you have to leave room for the veneer, which is glued to its outer face.

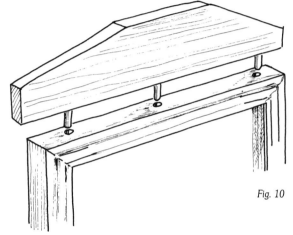

Fig. 10

With the top extension in place, hold it there and carefully shoot the joints each side for the narrow strips that extend down the sides of the frame. Wrap cling film around the top of the frame. Fit and glue the extension pieces to the top, holding them in place with masking tape (Fig. 11).

Fig. 11

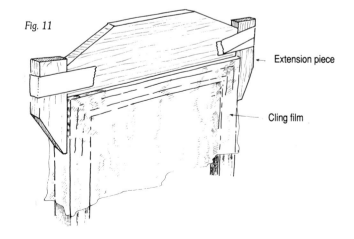

Extension piece

Cling film

Repeat at the bottom, fitting the central part first and then the two side pieces.

When the glue is dry, smooth the joints. Then roughen the face of the extension pieces with the teeth of the tenon or hack saw.

Applying the veneer

Select some pieces of mahogany veneer. You can arrange the grain of the veneer so that it is parallel with the grain of the extension pieces – that is, vertically – or you can cut the veneer and arrange the pieces so that they appear to radiate from the centre of the mirror.

If you decide to cut the veneers, use a sharp craft knife (or adapt a steel-bladed table knife by filing fine teeth in its rounded end) and bear it against a straightedge (Fig 12).

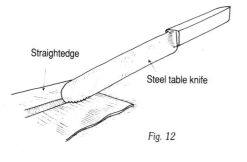

Straightedge

Steel table knife

Fig. 12

You can apply veneer in a number of ways. Small areas such as these can be held down using a thixotropic contact adhesive, such as Evostick, which you apply to both surfaces, and press together when the glue has gone tacky. The advantage of this glue is that it does not contain moisture and so is unlikely to cause the backing piece or the veneer to buckle. Its disadvantage is that the joint between the veneer and the backing is not close, and so you might find that the veneer splits away from the backing as you saw the extension pieces to shape.

Alternatively, you can glue down the veneer using woodworker's white PVA glue. Because this is water-based it will cause the veneer and the backing to swell and distort, and a considerable amount of pressure will be needed to keep them flat.

To minimize distortion, you can apply a layer of glue to the back of the extension piece, which will help to keep it flat while the glue dries. A more satisfactory system is to apply a backing veneer to the reverse of the extension pieces at the same time as you glue on the facing veneer, and this will give you a very strong sandwich construction (Fig 13).

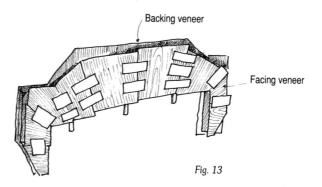

Backing veneer

Facing veneer

Fig. 13

A further point is worth noting. If for various reasons you have laid the veneer horizontally – that is, parallel with the top of the mirror rather than vertical to it – you might find that the veneer pulls and warps the extension pieces. To avoid this you will either have use a non-water-based glue to hold the veneer or apply a counter-veneer beneath the facing veneer, with its grain at right angles to that of the veneer on top of it. This will help hold the extension piece flat (Fig 14).

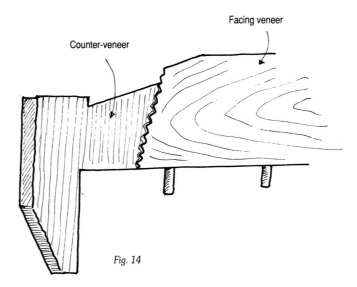

Fig. 14

Whichever of these methods you choose, you will find that veneering flat surfaces as small as these is straightforward and that the decorative benefits are well worth the extra trouble involved.

Tape the pieces of veneer together with masking tape. Spread copious amounts of glue to the face of the extension piece – you cannot have too much – then carefully lower the veneer on to it. Press out the surplus glue and, when you are sure that it is correctly positioned and unlikely to slip around when pressure is applied, spread cling film, then a couple of sheets of newspaper over it, or a sheet of felt underlay.

Sandwich it between flat boards and clamp them together (Fig 15).

When the glue has dried and you have peeled off the news-paper, trim away waste veneer at the edges, and scrape the

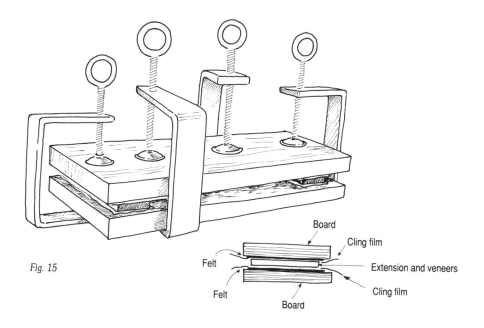

Fig. 15

Board
Cling film
Felt
Extension and veneers
Cling film
Felt
Board

veneer clean. Use a cabinet scraper for this and hold it almost vertically to limit its cut. Sand the veneer flat and smooth with 180 grit paper.

Cutting the extension pieces

Using the squared drawings in the plans, make a full-size template of the top and bottom extension pieces. Cut them out with a sharp knife and draw them on the mahogany veneer.

Take the top extension piece, fit a heavy blade to your fret saw and cut around the top profile. (For instructions on using a fret saw see pages 149–50.) If you find it more difficult than you expected, practise on some scraps before continuing. Remember that when you use a fret saw, the blade moves vertically and you have to feed the wood into the blade. When you come to a sharp turn, keep the blade moving and turn the wood to reposition it for the next cut, but do not feed it into the blade until the wood is lined up properly.

When both pieces have been cut, they can be glued to the frame. For the best finish though, it is sensible to keep them separate and polish them before joining them together. This will enable you to stain and polish the frame and the extensions without having to cope with awkward corners and obstructions.

Staining

Use Colron stains or naphtha-based stains obtainable from Fiddes & Son, Cardiff. Apply the stains with a cotton rag in the direction of the grain. Stain the sides of the mirror frame and the edges of the extension pieces. Leave them to dry.

Filling

Cabinet-makers' suppliers will be able to supply a good quality grain filler. You should buy a filler that is the same colour as the wood you have stained. Apply a thin coat of shellac over the wood, wipe it on with a bunched-up rag or brush it on thinly. Leave the shellac to dry and then rub the filler into the grain with a rag dipped in the filler paste. Clean off the excess immediately with a light and brisk cross-grain rubbing action using a dry cloth. Try to keep the rags neat, so that they do not catch on the prongs and curls of the decorative woodwork.

Leave the filler to dry, then brush another thin coat of shellac over it to seal it.

Finishing the frame

Mouldings are awkward to polish, and the simplest and probably the best finish is to apply one or two coats of varnish to it.

Choose a good quality varnish, apply the varnish slowly and leave the frame to dry in a clean and – as far as you can arrange it – dust-free room.

Give the varnish plenty of time to dry. Varnishes harden on the surface long before the interior gums have gone off. When you are sure the varnish is hard, take a small wad of cotton wool, about enough to make a table tennis ball when it is scrunched up hard, and wrap it in a small square of clean cotton, twisting the cotton to hold and compress the wool (Fig. 16). Open up the cotton, and drop a dozen or so drips of button polish on to the wool. Close the cotton again. Press the mop against your hand, until you can feel and see the polish squeezing through.

Now sprinkle a little pumice powder, whiting or other fine abrasive on to the damp patch of the mop and one or two small drops of linseed oil. Lightly and evenly, draw the mop around the moulding. The abrasive will cut back and smooth the moulding, and the polish will impart a hard glitter to it. After a few times around, leave the frame for the polish to harden.

Fig. 16

Problems with applying polish
- If the mop drags and pulls up the varnish, the varnish is not hard enough.

- If the mop sticks and pulls as you try to move it along, you are not using enough lubrication oil.

- If the mop slides and skids or if there is a fine cloudy residue left on the frame, you have used too much oil. Wipe the frame dry, re-charge the mop with polish and try again, adding more oil very sparingly and only when necessary.

Finishing the extensions
A French polish finish is best here. Make the mop described above, and charge it with plenty of button polish, and wrap it in the twist of cotton cloth.

Hold the mop as shown in Fig. 17 and use it in a circular motion, applying increasing pressure as the supply of polish dwindles. Do not press hard to begin with, or you will leave ridges in the finish that will be difficult to hide.

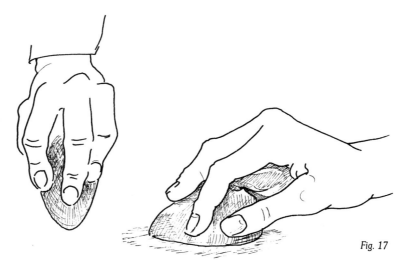

Fig. 17

After a short while, you will find that the polish solvent (methylated spirits) is softening the existing finish and spoiling it. There should be a slight pull to the mop, but not one that leaves a torn or uneven path behind the mop. If you suspect this is beginning to happen, you can either leave the work to harden and recommence the next day, or you can dab a drop of raw linseed oil on to the face of the mop and continue. This will leave a tail of fine mist on the wood, rather like the tail of shooting star, which will die out about 4in (100mm) from the mop. You can carry on covering and smoothing the faces of the two extensions now, until you have built up a sealed and smooth finish. If you are impatient and go on for too long though, you will find the finish becomes unstable and difficult to keep smooth. As the finish improves, change your hand action from circles to long ovals, and then finish with vertical swoops of the mop, leaving the extension at the end of each swoop. Stop to let the work harden, but before leaving it, lightly wipe away any oil clouds left on its surface.

FINISHING

Wait until the coating has hardened, and then mix up a mixture of 50 per cent button polish to 50 per cent methylated spirits. Charge a new mop with this and delicately apply finishing strokes up and down the extensions, starting and finishing each stroke off the wood.

This should remove any remaining oil, and bring the polish to a high, burnished gloss. Leave the work to harden, and then scatter pumice powder over the extensions and wipe them lightly with a soft cloth. This will remove the hard gloss, and the extensions will be ready for waxing.

Assembly

Before waxing, assemble the mirror. Glue the dowels in the extension into the frame and support the joints right round the frame with small wood blocks.

Gilding

Although you do not need to, gilding the concave part of the frame (which is right next to the glass) with gold leaf, looks really good. Transfer gold leaf is obtainable from good cabinet-makers' suppliers. You will also need some gold size, which is a good quality, slow-drying, oil-based varnish.

Take a small, soft brush and paint the concave part of the moulding evenly and sparingly with the gold size. Leave the gold size until it goes tacky. It might be a help if you apply some size to an offcut of smooth finished wood, so that you can experiment with the following procedure.

Check the gold size. Press your finger against the size, which should be tacky, and when you remove your finger, it should be dry. When it is like this, it is time to apply the gold. Take a sheet of gold leaf and press a corner of the gold foil against the tacky size. Lightly rub the backing paper with a finger nail or a soft pencil to help it to adhere to the size. Remove the paper – you should have left a section of gold behind, glued to the size.

Take a soft, dry brush and brush it across the gold. If the gold moves, snags or goes dull, you must wait a little longer before applying more gold.

Continue around the frame. If some areas of the gold look greasy after they have been applied leave the work for a while. This happens when the size is still too wet and is soaking through the leaf. You will need to leave it a while for the size to harden. An extra layer of gold leaf to cover blemishes can be applied once the first coat of gold size has gone completely hard.

Once the leaf is applied, work around the frame, pressing the gold into the moulding with a small wad of cotton wool, and then dust away any excess gold. Later, when the gold size has dried, brush a thin coat of warm, clear size over the gold, to improve its lustre and to protect it.

Fitting the mirror

The mirror glass fits into the rebate of the frame. Order the mirror slightly smaller than the rebate.. Lay the mirror frame face down and lay the mirror in the rebate. Fold a sheet of brown paper behind the mirror and then lay the backing plank into the rebate. Turn the mirror over, to check that the glass lies flat against the gilt frame, and then turn it back. Hold the plank with a few pins, knocked into the frame with the side of a heavy chisel, and fit glue blocks around the inside edge of the back frame, gluing them between the frame and the backing plank.

Fit some heavy screw eyes to the back of the frame, and use brass picture wire to suspend the mirror.

BOOKCASE

This is a copy of an old oak bookcase that we bought from an antique shop in a small village in Herefordshire. The original is hand planed, and its surfaces are contorted and undulating. I have tried to reproduce this effect. I used partially seasoned oak for the sides and shelves, and asked a carpenter to thickness it to a little over ⅝in (15mm). The surfaces were then hand planed and sanded to remove the machining marks. As the wood has dried out, it has shrunken unevenly. The knots and areas of dense grain have shrunk less than the open, clear-grained areas, and, to a limited extent, I have achieved the look I was aiming for. As time goes by there will be more movement, and this will further enhance the bookcase.

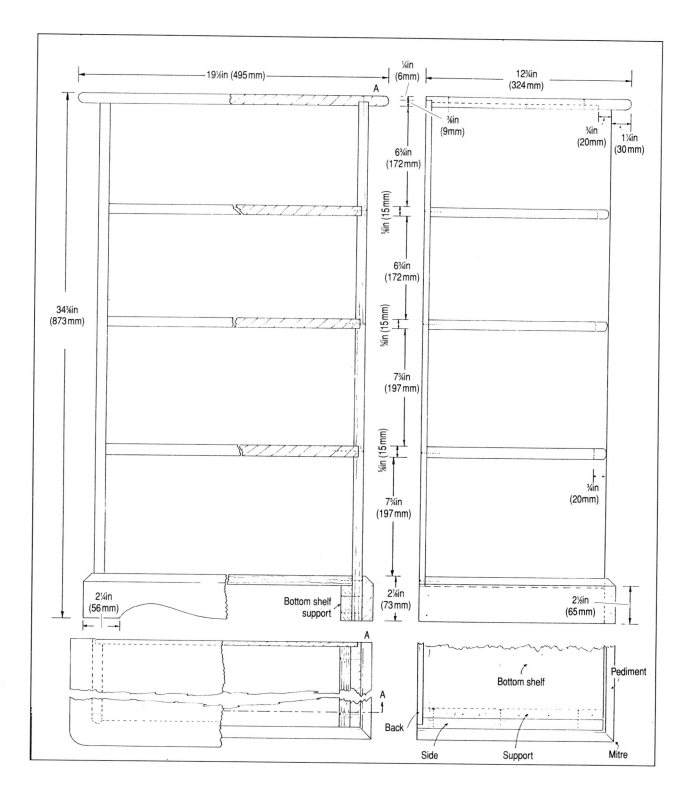

19½in (495mm)

¼in (6mm)

12¾in (324mm)

A

⅜in (9mm)

¾in (20mm)

1¼in (30mm)

6¾in (172mm)

⅝in (15mm)

6¾in (172mm)

⅝in (15mm)

7¾in (197mm)

⅝in (15mm)

7¾in (197mm)

¾in (20mm)

34⅜in (873mm)

2⅞in (73mm)

2¼in (56mm)

Bottom shelf support

2½in (65mm)

A

A

Bottom shelf

Pediment

Back

Side

Support

Mitre

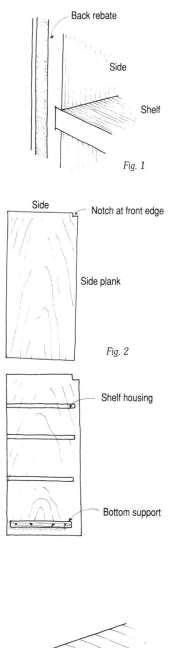

Fig. 1

Fig. 2

Fig. 5

CONSTRUCTION

Cut all the components to size. Note that the three top shelves finish ⅜in (9mm) short of the front of the sides and the same amount at the back to accommodate the back planking (Fig. 1). The back planking is nailed against the back edges of the shelves. The front edge of the bottom shelf is left square and lies flush with the sides. As you will expect, the top and sides have a ⅜in (9mm) rebate at the back to hold the back planks.

Mark out the sides first, using the bottom edges as the reference point. Cut the tops square. Mark and cut the notches at the tops to conceal the ends of the housings (Fig. 2), then mark the positions for the three housed shelves, and the position for the top of the shelf support at the bottom. This should be 2 ⅞in (73mm) up from the bottom edge, less the thickness of the bottom shelf (Fig. 3).

Make the simple template described on pages 91–2, which bears against the router guide plate, for routing out the housings. Fit the guide plate to the bed of the router and rout out the housings.

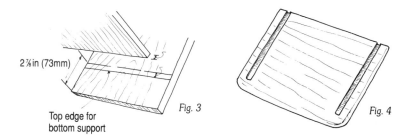

Fig. 3

Fig. 4

Now cut out the top. Saw the sides and front square, and mark the positions for the two housings that hold the sides (Fig. 4). Use the same template guide for routing out these two housings.

While you are still using the router, remove the guide plate and fit the parallel guide. Rout out the rebates at the back edges of the sides and the back underside edge of the top. Cut the radii at the front corners of the top, using a coping saw or a jig saw, and then use a chisel to round off the edges. Finish with a shoulder plane, file and sandpaper.

Cut out the shelves, remembering that the bottom shelf is narrower than the others (by the depth of the housings) and deeper. Saw out the notches in the upper three shelves, and round their front edges (Fig. 5). Leave the front edge of the bottom shelf square.

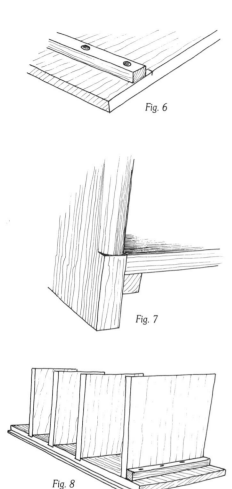

Fig. 6

Fig. 7

Fig. 8

Fig. 9

Nail and glue the bottom shelf supports on the inside edge of the sides (Fig. 6). Pencil in the exact position of the upper edge of the bottom shelf on the front edges of the sides, and from that point upwards round off the front edges (Fig. 7).

Fit all the pieces together. When you know that they fit, glue and nail the bottom shelf to its support, and glue the other shelves to one side. Run a little glue on the ends of the shelves, and rest the side on top of the shelves. Tap the shelves into their housings (Fig. 8). Slip the top into position and clamp the two sides together at the base.

When you have aligned the bottom shelf with the front edge of the side, tighten the clamp and nail the shelf in position.

Take some 1½in (38mm) oval nails and nail the top into the sides. Drive a couple of nails into each end of each shelf. Fit a diagonal batten at the front of the bookcase to hold the sides and bottom square, and then tack the backboards or plywood sheet into the rebates at the sides and top, and against the back edges of the shelves.

Make up a strip of moulding for the pediment, and plane the bevel at its top.

The pediment is mitred at the front corners, and nailed to the front edge of the sides, and to the edge of the bottom shelf (Fig. 9).

Cut the mitres, and then saw out the simple frieze at its bottom edge. (Instructions for cutting mitres are on pages 95–7.) Fit the mitres on the return mouldings. Nail and glue the front moulding before nailing and gluing the side mouldings. Fill all the nail holes, and sand the bookcase before staining it.

FINISHING

This bookcase is made from oak. After sanding, we brushed tannic acid on to the outside and inside of the bookcase and left it to dry. After a little more sanding, we applied our masking fluid (tomato ketchup) to the sides and to part of the top (see pages 50-1) and fumed the bookcase in a polythene bag with a dish of ammonia. We opened the bag after 4 hours and were disappointed to find the masking had been less effective than expected. This was probably due to the application of ketchup being thinner than that used on the joint stool. After cleaning up the bookcase, we stained it with a mixture of English Light Oak, Canadian Cedar and a dash of American Walnut stains and finished with a brushed coat of shellac, wire wool and wax.

THE WORKSHOP

Marking gauge

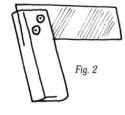

Fig. 1

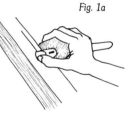

Fig. 1a

A marking gauge (Fig.1) is held and used as illustrated in Fig. 1a. When you are using a marking gauge, tilt it slightly so that the scriber is trailing behind the stock and make sure that the fence is pressed tightly against the timber you are marking. Marking gauges are usually held with one hand, but if you find this difficult at first, hold the wood in the vice and control the gauge with both hands.

Set square

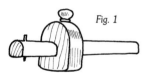

Fig. 2

A set square is used to check whether two adjacent flat surfaces are at right angles to each other (Fig. 2). It is used as illustrated in Fig. 3, and when you have found two sides that are planed square, mark them with the identifying marks.

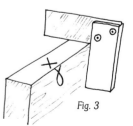

Fig. 3

Angle bevel

Fig. 4

An angle bevel, which is adjustable, is used for marking and checking other angles (Fig. 4). If you only have one angle bevel, and need to make several adjustments to it, record the previous angles on a spare block of wood (Fig. 5).

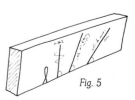

Fig. 5

SAWS

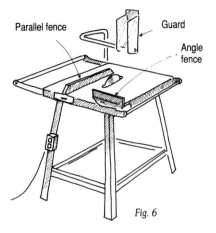

Parallel fence

Guard

Angle fence

Fig. 6

Circular saw

The circular saw is used for making straight saw cuts (Fig. 6). There are usually two fences available on the table. The parallel fence lies parallel with the saw blade, and it is for making cuts parallel to the edge of the plank. The angle fence bears against a side of the workpiece and guides it into the blade making a cross-grain saw cut.

SAFETY

- Always work deliberately while the saw blade is spinning.

- Never start the saw until the fences are adjusted and the wood is ready for sawing.

- Use sticks to press the work sideways against the fence and into the blade.

- Whenever possible, use the safety guard, which covers the blade, and wear goggles and ear muffs.

- Always arrange excellent lighting when you are using the saw. A single fluorescent tube emits a flickering light, which will make the rotating saw appear, at times, to be stationary. This stroboscopic effect is very dangerous, particularly if the saw is being used in this light for long periods. To eliminate the effect, fit a second tube, or use alternative lights when using the circular saw.

BLADES

Circular saws can be fitted with a range of blades. Multiple-toothed, tungsten-tipped blades are recommended; they stay sharp and are quieter than high-speed steel blades. If your saw table has a rise and fall adjustment, set the blade so that it protrudes by no more than ¼in (6mm) above the top surface of the wood being cut. This should result in a clean, relatively chip-free saw cut.

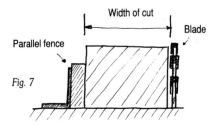

Width of cut

Blade

Parallel fence

Fig. 7

FENCES

Avoid using the circular saw without using the fences. These control the direction of the cut and prevent the saw from snatching or jamming. Set up the parallel fence for making parallel saw cuts, remembering to include in your calculations the width of the saw cut when you are adjusting the fence (Fig. 7). For

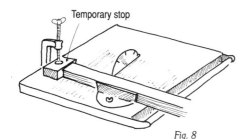
Temporary stop

Fig. 8

angled cross-cuts, use the adjustable guide. Where possible, hold the wood against the fence with one hand only and allow the fence to control and steady the work. This will help to prevent the saw from jamming. If a number of components of the same length are to be cut using the angled guide, set up a fence, as illustrated in Fig. 8, which locates the wood before it is sawn. If the parallel fence is used instead, the sawn-off pieces might jam or be thrown off the table by the revolving blade.

Jig saw

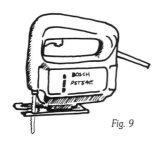

Fig. 9

This versatile tool (Fig. 9) is ideal for cutting curves in wood up to about 2½in (65mm) thick. A good quality jig saw, equipped with an orbital action, can be used for accurate straight cuts and sizing. Those fitted with an orbital cutting action cut more quickly and are easier to control. Speed control is an advantage when starting a cut or working in thin woods.

SAFETY

- Always clamp or support your work in the vice, allowing room for the blade underneath.

- Keep both hands on the tool: one hand controls the speed of the cut, the other its direction.

- Never allow your hands to stray under the workpiece and keep the electric cord well away from the blade.

BLADES

There is a great variety of blades available for the jig saw illustrated here. The blades that you will find the most useful are the T144D for cutting straight lines and the T111C for cutting curves in wood up to about 2¼in (56mm) thick.

Fig. 10

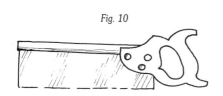

Tenon saw and hand saw

If you do not already possess a tenon saw, choose a small one, with a brass rather than a steel stiffening bar along the top of the blade (Fig. 10). Hold the saw as illustrated (Fig. 11), with the first finger resting against the side of the handle. Use the tenon saw in conjunction with the bench hook and mitre block, illustrated in Figs. 12 and 13. These are easily made in the workshop. For making a clean and accurate-across-the grain saw cut, incise the cutting line with a knife, chisel away a thin slice of wood on the waste side of the line and start off the saw in the resulting groove (Figs. 13a and 13b).

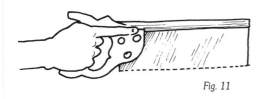

Fig. 11

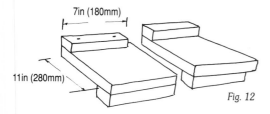
7in (180mm)

11in (280mm)

Fig. 12

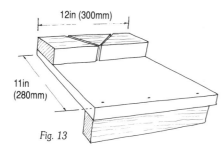

12in (300mm)

11in (280mm)

Fig. 13

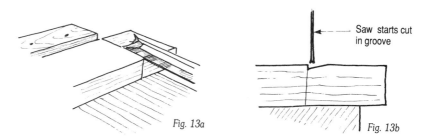

Saw starts cut in groove

Fig. 13a

Fig. 13b

For sawing down the cheek of a tenon, start with the saw at 45 degrees to the wood, and, as the depth of the cut increases, slowly bring the blade square with the side of the wood (Figs. 14–16).

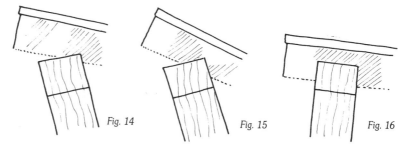

Fig. 14

Fig. 15

Fig. 16

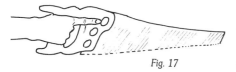

Fig. 17

Use a hand saw (Fig. 17) for cutting the cheeks of large tenons, and for long accurate sawcuts.

Most tool shops and ironmongers offer a saw-sharpening service, which you should use when your saw becomes difficult to control or blunt.

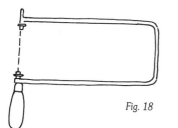

Fig. 18

Fret saw

This fine-bladed saw is used for delicate work (Fig. 18). The fret saw is invariably used with the home-made table, illustrated in Fig. 19.

The fret saw is a lightweight, delicate tool with a fine blade, which can cut intricate shapes in thin wood. Blades are usually obtained in a pack that contains a variety of blades with different tooth sizes, but for cutting the extension pieces around the mirror (see page 137), you will need the biggest size.

The saw cuts on the down stroke. Fit the blade with the teeth pointing downwards. Fit the blade in the bottom clamp nearest the handle first. You might find it necessary to tighten the wing nut with a pair of pliers or a small screwdriver. Loosen the top tensioning wing nut and, pressing the frame of the saw against the bench, feed the top of the blade into the top clamp and

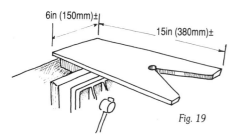

6in (150mm)±

15in (380mm)±

Fig. 19

Fig. 20

tighten it. Tension the blade with the top wing nut. The blade should be tight and ring when you pluck it.

The saw is held by the handle, with the saw frame tucked under the arm. Only a gentle vertical motion from the arm is required to make it cut (Fig. 20). About 2in (50mm) movement is all that is needed; more than this might stress the blade and break it. In this position it is impossible to steer the saw, because the frame is prevented from moving by your shoulder and arm. The work has to be fed and steered into the blade by the left hand.

To make this easier, nail together the simple saw table illustrated in Fig. 18. Hold it in the vice so that it projects beyond the bench. Hold the work at the apex of the V and keep the saw blade moving inside the circle. Practise on some waste wood, remembering to feed the wood slowly and to keep the saw blade moving, even when turning a sharp corner.

Coping saw

This saw (Fig. 21) has coarser teeth than the fret saw. The blade is held in tension by the sprung saw frame. The angle of the blade relative to the frame is adjusted by the swivels at each end of the blade. This saw is held with both hands, with the blade usually oriented to cut on the push stroke.

Fig. 21

PLANES

Two planes are illustrated here. The smoothing plane (Fig. 22), which is the larger of the two, is useful for general work. The shoulder or block plane (Fig. 23), which is fitted with a low angle-blade, is used for delicate work, particularly cross- and end-grain planing.

Fig. 22

Fig. 23

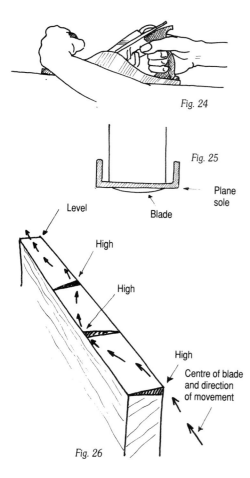

Fig. 24

Fig. 25

Plane sole

Blade

Level

High

High

High

Centre of blade and direction of movement

Fig. 26

Using a plane

Hold the plane with two hands. The left hand holds the knob at the front of the plane, and applies a slight downward pressure. The right hand propels the plane forwards (Fig. 24). If you practise this deliberate action, particularly as the plane enters and leaves the cut, you will be able plane a straight edge.

To plane an edge at right angles to a side, you will have to practise moving the plane from side to side as you push it forwards. Fig. 25 shows a typical (but exaggerated) cutting profile of a plane blade. It is obvious that the blade will cut slightly more wood at its centre than at its sides. By trailing a finger from each hand you can steer the tool to take advantage of this angled cut. Provided the sole of the plane is always pressed flat against the workpiece and you plan before each cut the line the blade should take, you will quickly learn how to square up a piece of wood (Fig. 26).

Planing end-grain

Use the shoulder plane for planing end-grain. The difficulty with end-grain is that the wood at the end of each plane stroke splinters. Set the blade to minimum cut and lubricate the sole of the plane with wax.

Take one of the following precautions to prevent the wood splintering:

- Plane the ends of a plank before trimming the sides. This way you can cut off the splintered wood after the end-grain has been planed (Fig. 27).

- Plane from both ends towards the middle (Fig. 28).

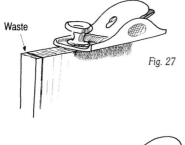

Waste

Fig. 27

Fig. 28

Fig. 29

- Arrange a sacrificial block, to press against the end of the piece being trimmed. If this piece splits, it can be discarded (Fig. 29).

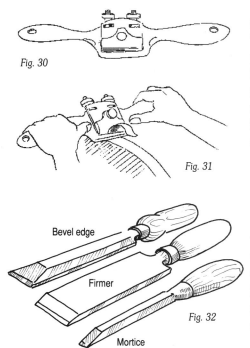

Fig. 30

Fig. 31

Spokeshave

The spokeshave (Fig. 30) is held with two hands, and drawn towards you (Fig. 31). The depth of cut is controlled by the knurled screws which hold the blade. When you are adjusting the blade, or after sharpening it, withdraw the blade with the two screws, and then gradually wind them in, keeping the blade in contact with the screws. Tighten the clamping iron against the blade to help hold it in position.

CHISELS

You will need one or two morticing chisels – ⅜in (9mm) and ½in (12mm) wide – and three bevel-edged chisels – ⅝in (15mm), ⅜in (9mm) and ¼in (6mm) wide (Fig. 32). Bevel-edged chisels are not tough tools. They should always be sharp and handled with delicacy. A 1½in (38mm) firmer chisel will also be useful.

Hold the chisel as illustrated in Fig. 33, and use both hands to control it. Rather than pushing the chisel with your arms, apply your body weight to press the chisel into the wood.

Bevel edge

Firmer

Fig. 32

Mortice

SAFETY

Chisels are easier and safer to use if they are sharp. Instructions for sharpening edge tools are on page 153. Remember to keep all your body (including your fingers!) behind the edge of the chisel, and make sure that the workpiece is fixed firmly before you start work.

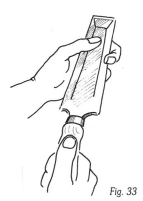

Fig. 33

GOUGES

These are held and used in the same way as chisels. Gouges are substantial tools and can be hit with a mallet. If you do not have a woodcarving mallet, find a short length of 2in (50mm) diameter branch that has been cut for firewood and use that instead. Square carpenter's mallets are heavy and cumbersome. As with a chisel, you should almost always aim to remove a shaving with each pass of the gouge. When you first use the gouge, practise the slight scooping motion that lifts the cutting edge out of the wood (Fig. 34).

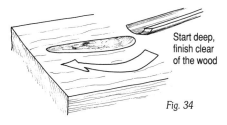

Start deep, finish clear of the wood

Fig. 34

SHARPENING

Edge tools

The instructions here are for sharpening edge tools – knives, chisels, plane blades and gouges.

First, you must recognize when your tools are blunt. Sometimes this is going to be obvious: the tool may have a gashed edge, highlighted if you hold the tip towards a strong light source, or the cutter may leave scratch marks as it slices through the wood. If you are careful in picking your tools up and placing them back on the bench, these gross faults will be quite uncommon. It is more likely that you will simply find a job harder work than you anticipated. If so, you must check the blade.

If you are using a chisel, try to slice off the corner of an offcut with a vertical chop (Fig. 35). It should be easy. If it is not, sharpen the blade. If you are using a penknife or a plane, hold a piece of paper against the edge of the blade, and slice slowly into the paper. If the knife cleaves through the paper cleanly the blade is sharp. If the paper tears or the knife hesitates, it is blunt.

Fig. 36 shows the angles at which you should try to sharpen your blades. You will need a medium and a fine oilstone and a leather strop. To sharpen gouges, you will also need to buy a curved slip stone.

The sharpening procedure is as follows:

* Lubricate the medium oilstone.

* Hold the blade as illustrated in Fig. 37, with its sharpening bevel flat against the oilstone, and grind it along the stone, keeping the blade at a constant angle.

* Repeat this five times or until you raise a slight roughness at the tip of the blade (Fig. 38).

* Turn over the blade, hold it flat against the stone and push it forward. This will grind off the burr.

* Do this once, then repeat the first stage, keeping the tool at the same angle as before, but pressing more gently.

* Remove the burr and repeat once more.

* Now lubricate the fine oilstone and repeat the whole process a few more times.

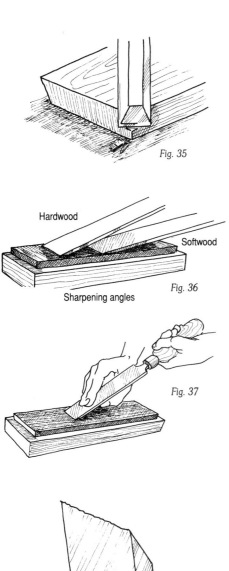

Fig. 35

Hardwood

Softwood

Fig. 36

Sharpening angles

Fig. 37

Fig. 38

Finish by using the strop. You can usually buy stropping compound from a gentleman's barber. There are normally two grades of compound in the package. Rub the compounds on to two strips of leather. They are usually different colours, so it will be easy to distinguish which leather strip is which.

Then, repeating the process described above, drag the sharpening bevel five times down the strop, then once more with the blade flat against the leather to remove the burr.

Repeat on the finest compound. If you look closely at the mark left by the blade on the strop you will be able to tell whether you have succeeded in obtaining a good edge. If the blade leaves a row of fine parallel lines you will have to return to the fine stone to remove the minute knicks that have remained in the blade.

Once you have obtained a good edge, do your best to preserve it. Take care picking up and putting down your tools. Never, for example, place a plane flat on the workbench. Strop your tools regularly.

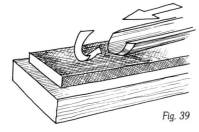

Fig. 39

Gouges

Gouges are sharpened in the same way, except that you will have to apply a rolling action to the tool as you grind the outside bevel (Fig. 39). If you grind the outside bevel on the flat surface of the slip stone, you will slowly form a groove. Use the same groove every time; as it deepens, more of the curved edge will be ground at each pass of the gouge. Remove the burr every five strokes with the slipstone, as illustrated in Fig. 40.

Make the stropping board shown in Fig. 41. Rub compound into the grooves made by the tools and use the board as a finishing strop.

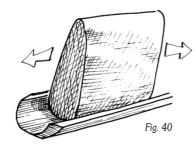

Fig. 40

Cabinet scraper

A cabinet scraper is a straight-sided thin plate of hard steel (Fig. 42). It is held as illustrated (Fig. 43), and drawn or pushed along the grain of a piece of wood to smooth it. It works best on hard,

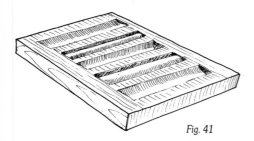

Fig. 41

Fig. 43

Fig. 42

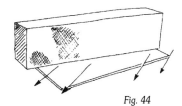

Fig. 44

dense woods. A fine hook is worked on both edges of each side. this removes a fine shaving as it is drawn across the timber.

To sharpen a cabinet scraper, grind off any traces of a previous burr with an oilstone (Fig. 44). Clamp it in the vice, as illustrated, then take a fine, flat file and, holding it on the edge of the scraper, remove the used edge (Fig. 45). File carefully until the new edge is flat and hard-edged. Now, take the back of

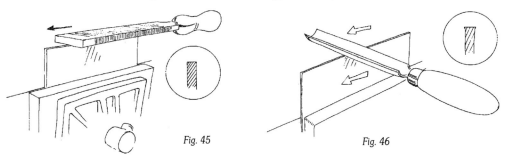

Fig. 45   Fig. 46

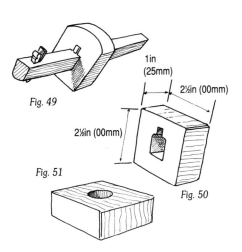

Fig. 47

Fig. 48

a gouge or shank of a screwdriver as a burnishing iron, and draw it once or twice along the edge (Fig. 46). Follow with a couple of light strokes along each side to form the hook. After a little use, the scraper will lose its edge, and you can then turn it around and use a new corner.

When all four have been used, run the point of a pair of compasses along the edge to clean and lift it (Fig. 47), then stroke a new hook with the burnishing tool as illustrated in Fig. 48. The edge can be restored only once or twice before it is necessary to file a new edge and form new hooks.

HOME-MADE TOOLS

Gauges

You will need several marking gauges (Fig. 49). Even second-hand gauges are quite expensive to buy, but they are easy to make and it is worth making one or two for yourself.

Choose some small offcuts of hardwood – pear, sycamore or beech are satisfactory; oak and African mahogany are ideal. Cut out the fence to the dimensions shown (Fig. 50), find the centre on each side and drill through the middle with a ¾in (20mm) bit. This drill hole should be perpendicular to the face side, and if you do not have a drill stand, drill in from both sides (Fig. 51).

Fig. 49

1in
(25mm)

2½in (00mm)

2½in (00mm)

Fig. 50

Fig. 51

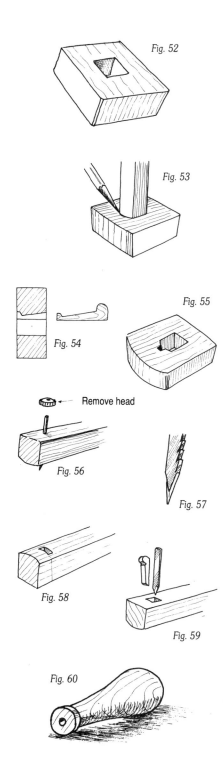

Fig. 52

Fig. 53

Fig. 55

Fig. 54

Remove head

Fig. 56

Fig. 57

Fig. 58

Fig. 59

Fig. 60

Next use a set square to mark sides of the square-sided hole required for the stock, and cut back to the line very carefully with a chisel, again working from both sides and meeting at the centre (Fig. 52).

Cut out the stock, make it a slightly rectangular in section – ¾ × ⅞in (20 × 22mm). It needs to be a very firm fit, so although the bigger dimension should not fit the existing hole in the fence, check as you trim the ¾in (20mm) sides to make sure you do not plane it too narrow.

Plane a slight radius on the upper edge of the stock, position it over the hole (Fig. 53) and pencil on both sides of the fence the curve you have made. Use a gouge to carve away the waste, until the stock is a tight sliding fit.

The stock is held with a wedge. This is located in the fence by a key-way, which can easily be cut with a fine chisel. Fit a thin wooden wedge into the key-way. If you follow the design suggested here (Fig. 54), the wedge will stay put even when it is tapped loose. Finish the fence by drawing a curve on its top, and smooth it to the shape illustrated (Fig. 55).

Mark and drill a hole for the marking point. A picture hanging nail makes a good point, and it should be a very tight fit in the stock (Fig. 56).

If you want to make this into a cutting gauge, grind a suitable blade to size. A jig saw blade will do well, and it should be ground and honed as illustrated in Fig. 57.

To fit it, mark the position for the blade on the top and bottom of the stock, and drill through the stock at the end marks of the blade (Fig. 58). Use a fret saw to remove the waste between the drill holes, and then square up the hole with a narrow rat-tailed file.

If you are using a jig saw blade and can make the slot a tight fit, you will be able to dispense with a wedge to hold the cutter. If your hole is a little big, then you should chisel a slot for a wedge on the outer end of the stock (Fig. 59).

Making chisels and gouges

Carving tools are expensive, and it is worth making your own tools when your regular collection of chisels cannot do the work you need.

Make the handles from any block of hardwood. Smooth it and taper its grip as shown in Fig. 60. If you have a lathe and are turning one, turn several more and keep them ready for when you might need them. Bore a hole into the end of each handle. It should be slightly smaller in diameter than the steel that will be driven into it.

Make the blade from silver steel, which you can buy in various sections and sizes from any good tool store. To save yourself a lot of tedious filing, buy sections that are a little smaller than the cutting edge you need and expect to hammer your tools to the required shape. Cut the steel to length. You will want about 5in (127mm) of steel for the blade and a further 2in (50mm) to poke into the handle.

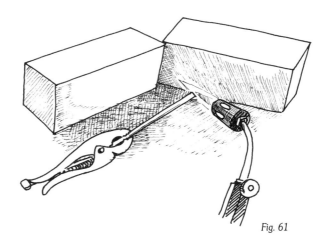

Fig. 61

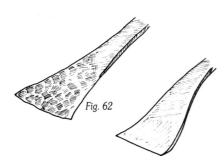

Fig. 62

Arrange a couple of fire bricks (Fig. 61), and use a gas torch to heat the tip of the steel to a bright, cherry red. Hold the other end of the steel with a wrench. When the end is hot enough, hammer the tip against an anvil or a heavy metal block until it is the shape you require. You will probably have to use the torch several times to re-heat the end before you are satisfied with the shape you have beaten (Fig. 62). File the blade to the exact shape you want.

Heat the other end, and beat it to a point. To harden the blade, heat it up again until it glows cherry red, and while it is still bright red, plunge the tool into a dish of cold cooking oil. Hold the shank of the blade in the vice with its point sticking up, and heat the point with the blow torch. When it is glowing red hot, place the handle over the point, and tap it down with a hammer. You can now clean up the blade with some emery paper, and hone it to a fine edge with sharpening stones.

SUPPLIERS

Most of the materials and tools required to make the pieces of furniture featured in this book can be obtained from your local hardware store, but I include a short list of specialist companies which you might find useful. They have a thorough knowledge of their speciality, and are always able to give useful advice. Their service is prompt and reasonably priced.

Wood
Interesting Timbers, Hazel Farm, Compton Martin, Somerset BS18 6LH

Cabinet-Makers' Finishing Materials
Fiddes and Son Ltd, Florence Works, Brindley Road, Cardiff CF1 71X

Brassware
John Lawrence and Co. (Dover) Ltd, Granville Street, Dover, Kent CT16 2LF

Tools
Sarjents Tools, 44–52 Oxford Road, Reading, Berkshire RG1 7LH

The following American companies have been recommended to me

Wood
Maurice L. Condon Co. Inc., 248 Ferris Avenue, White Plains, NY 10603

Tools and Brassware
Woodcraft, 41 Atlantic Avenue, PO Box 4000, Woburn, MA 01888

INDEX